A portion of the profits from this book will be donated to Coaching the Global Village, a nonprofit organization that uses coaching to create innovative solutions to pressing global challenges. To learn more, please visit www.coachingtheglobalvillage.org.

COACHING *is* CALLING

A Guide to Coach Training Programs
and Professional Career Paths

LAUREN B. WEINSTEIN

Coaching is Calling: A Guide to Coach Training Programs and
Professional Career Paths
Lauren B. Weinstein

Copyright © 2014 by Lauren B. Weinstein
All Rights Reserved

Cover and Interior Design: Rebecca Pollock
Copyeditor: Ewurama Ewusi-Mensah
Proofreader: Jill Amack

All rights reserved. This book was self-published by the author, Lauren B. Weinstein. No part of this publication may be reproduced, distributed, or transmitted in any form or by any means, including photocopying, recording, or other electronic or mechanical methods, without the prior written permission of the author, except in the case of brief quotations embodied in critical reviews and certain other noncommercial uses permitted by copyright law. For permission requests, please contact the author at www.coachingiscalling.com.

Although the author has made every effort to ensure that the information in this book was correct at press time, the author does not assume and hereby disclaim any liability to any party for any loss, damage, or disruption caused by errors or omissions, whether such errors or omissions result from negligence, accident, or any other cause.

ISBN 978-1494730390

Version 1.0

This book is dedicated to the memory of Mr. Jack Morris, the kind of coach I aspire to be.

ACKNOWLEDGMENTS

This book is only possible because of the help I received from others.

My dad sent me a text message after I changed careers: "All successful people have had to take risks to get ahead… You have a passion, you have a plan, and you are able to make your life what you want it to be…it's exciting, empowering, and filled with opportunity." Mom and Dad, thank you for encouraging me to follow my own calling in life.

Daniel Sheres, my thought partner: I would not have been able to write this book without your constant source of brilliance. Thank you for helping me to develop my ideas and notice countless distinctions. Now it's time for you to focus on your own book!

Special thanks to Annie Frome, my coach and friend, whose input and support has been invaluable. Also, special thanks to Shelley Danner, my idea partner and dear friend, whose thoughtfulness and editing skills I am grateful for.

I want to thank the following individuals for spending time with me over the phone and email. You are a driving force behind this book, and I am grateful for your help in shaping my ideas and thoughts about coaching and coach training programs.

Thank you: Frank Ball, John Bennett, Terry Behrman, Stephanie Bohnett, Jason Bomberger, Robin Bowyer, Sue Bond, Bridgette Boudreau, Denise Bray, Dr. Vikki Brock, Renee Brotman, Sarah

Brooks, Rita Brown, Christine Calandrella, Clif Cannon, Eugene Chang, Rey Carr, Judy Clothier, Janet Crawford, Matthew Cross, Holly Denton, Eric de Nijs, Leslie Everheart, Angela (Angie) Feehan, Garry Fisher, Mary Kay Garrett, Cindy Grosser, Dave Hanna, Carla Hamby, Beatrice (Bebe) Hanson, Ruth Ann Harnisch, Wendy Johnson, Virginia Kellogg, Andrew (Andy) Kirschner, Judy Krings, Sheppard Lake, Carylynn (Cary) Larson, Pat Mathews, Christopher McAuliffe, Nancy McCaughey, Tom McLaughlin, Toni McLean, Micki McMillan, Natalie Tucker Miller, Magdalena (Magda) Mook, Mary Elizabeth Murphy, Junie Nathani, Jennifer (Jen) Ostrich, Tanisha Drummer Parrish, Jeffrey Platts, Suzi Pomerantz, Wendy Preyssler, Peter Reding, Val Rosettani, Garry Schleifer, Melissa Scott, Carol Shannon, Ann Stevens, Deb St. John, Michael Stratford, Anabel Suárez, Jennifer Voss, Laura Baehre Westman, Christine (Chris) Wahl, Debbie Weil, and Dr. Patrick Williams.

I am deeply grateful to my supportive friends and family. There are too many to name, however I would like to thank those who have helped me in specific and various ways as I wrote this book. Thank you: Marco Ambrosio, Dan Caroff, Stefanie Ginsburg, Katrina Gordon, Lee Jacobs, Noah Karesh, Curtis (Curt) Krasik, Katherine Kriegman, Victoria Lai, James Milin, Megan Schumann, and Brian Weinberg.

CONTENTS

Foreword by Daniel Sheres 1

Preface 5
    My Coaching Story 5

Introduction 13
    Why I Wrote This Book 15
    How to Read This Book 16
    Methodology 18
    A Word Before You Begin 19

Part I: Your Coaching Journey 21
    Worksheet: Why Coaching? Why Now? 22
    Do the Work on Yourself 28
    Create Your Own Developmental Path 32

Part II: What You Need to Know about Coaching 37
    Coaching 101 40
    Clients Have a Need 40
    Coaches Offer a Service 41
    How to Think about Coaching 42
    Responding to Clients' Issues or Immediate Needs 44
    Responding to Clients' Roles and Responsibilities 45
    Responding to Contexts or Phases of Clients' Lives 46
    Worksheet: What Kind of Clients Do You Want to Serve? .. 48
    Professional Opportunities and Career Paths 51
    Related Fields to Consider 54

Part III: What You Need to Know about Coach Training Programs 57

    Benefits of a Coach Training Program 60
    Coaching Certification and Reputation 63
    Different Approaches to Coaching 71
    Access to Coaching Colleagues 79
    A Continuous Learning Environment 84
    Focus on Developing Yourself 88
    Support to Launch a Coaching Business 91
    Program Logistics 92
    Investing in Your Coach Training 95

Part IV: Find the Coach Training Program that Best Fits Your Needs 101

    Do Your Research 104
    Interview Coaches and Program Staff 105
    Sample the Program 106
    Know When It Feels Right 107
    Worksheet: Guided Questions for Selecting a Coach Training Program 109

Part V: Coaching Resources 117

    Coaching Associations and Organizations 119
    Organizations that Support Coach Training/Education 128
    Websites and Magazines 129
    Books 132
    Coach Training Programs 133

Conclusion 139

About the Author 144

FOREWORD

COACHING IS CALLING

FOREWORD BY DANIEL SHERES

BECOMING A COACH IS YOUR WHOLE LIFE

In the spring of 2007, I was sitting around a table with several coaches. We were on a lunch break during a workshop on emotional intelligence. There were eight of us, and a variety of coaches were present: there was a life coach, a leadership coach, three executive coaches, a relationship coach, and a business coach. And then there was me. I was a management consultant at the time and just beginning to investigate the idea of becoming a coach. The conversation was focused around a simple question:

What makes a coach?

After talking through all the training workshops we had done, the degree and certification programs we had attended, the books we had read, the mentors we had, and on and on, it dawned on us:

Becoming a coach is your whole life.

This idea was at once so simple and so profound. The process of becoming a coach certainly involves dedicated training and learning. Yet it must also somehow engage the richness of our own personal experiences in such a way as to offer meaningful insights for others. I remember feeling a rush of excitement—as if I had been preparing to become a coach my whole life without knowing it and was finally being called into action, not because of something I could be, but because of something I already was, something I was perhaps even born to be.

Many coaches I know have experienced a similar revelation. Many of us have achieved great success despite significant challenges. Others have developed a deep and thorough understanding of transformation by careful observation and study. But what is common to all of us is that we are curious, thoughtful individuals by nature. We love to learn, grow, experiment, and question, and we revel in the discoveries we make along the way. On some fundamental level, coaching offers us the opportunity to put a dedicated intention behind this natural inclination. In becoming a coach each of us declares that the insights gained from life until now and the learnings we will gain from our training and experiences in the future are not just for ourselves. They are to be used in service to others.

It's important to recognize that your own journey to becoming a coach began years ago. Perhaps you have a knack for developing professional or personal relationships. Perhaps you were born with a capacity to empathize, understand, and listen. Perhaps you've been a trusted advisor for as long as you can remember. Perhaps your own work with a coach has empowered you toward greater levels of success, fulfillment, and clarity of purpose. And perhaps you are simply that insightful individual whose passion for self-inquiry demands to be shared.

You will have several opportunities throughout the book to pause and reflect on your own journey. For those of you who have never worked with a coach, it will be your introduction to the kind of self-observation we often ask of our clients. Pay special attention to the questions asked of you and take your time with them. There are no right or wrong answers and there is no one looking over your shoulder. The insights you gain will not only guide you toward the coach training program that is the best fit, they will help you to better understand and articulate your path to personal fulfillment and success as a coach. Simply answer the questions to the best of your ability. Then answer them again. Look deep within for the most authentic answers you can provide, and trust that the insights you gain will lead you perfectly toward the best training and career path for you.

Your path to becoming a coach has been your whole life. It continues with this book.

Daniel Sheres
October 16, 2013

PREFACE

MY COACHING STORY

When I graduated from the University of Pennsylvania in 2006, I kept telling my friends that my true calling was to be a coach. My dad, a successful eye surgeon, had worked with a career coach for years. He always attributed his ability to stay focused on his career and prioritize his relationships to his conversations with his coach.

I thought that being a coach sounded like the best job ever. I imagined sitting in my pajamas, headphones plugged into my phone, dispensing advice to people all around the world as I drank my morning chai tea. Or maybe I would live on a houseboat, stand-up paddle board every day, and swim with dolphins in between client calls.

As a coach I would be able to: a) work from anywhere, b) help people, and c) get paid for it. But with my limited work experience, I tucked that idea in my back pocket.

A couple of years later, I was ready for a change in my corporate job. I was working long hours for a client whose work did not energize me. It seemed like I had strayed far from my vision of myself, and I felt that I was going down the wrong path. I reached out to a life coach.

She recommended that I read *Conquering Your Quarterlife Crisis*, a book that focuses on the perspectives of twentysomethings who are unsure about their life direction. She had me complete a ten-page intake form that I faxed to her from a hotel in Chennai, India, where I was working in health IT. When the coach did not respond to me, I felt lost and confused. I expected more from a coach and vowed that, if I ever became a coach, I would be clear with my communications and commitments.

Fortunately, the self-reflection and reading she provided helped me become more aware of my desire to shift careers and gave me the patience to change. I was grateful for the brief encounter I'd had with coaching and for the book's impact on my own professional direction. As a result, I focused on exploring alternative career paths within the company I worked for and started to shift into corporate social responsibility and international development, two areas I am passionate about.

While working in international development for several years, I responded to proposals from nongovernmental organizations requesting consulting services. I also interviewed and vetted internal candidates who wanted to go on international assignments. While the organizations and programs we worked for empowered thousands of people miles away, I felt removed from the impact. I felt like I was making more of a difference to the individuals I interviewed to go on assignments than to the people we ultimately helped.

I continued to heed the advice of *Conquering Your Quarterlife Crisis* and gave myself the time to make deliberate and strategic shifts in my career. As I was continuously promoted and became more deeply entrenched in the do-good community at my company, peers, friends, and friends of friends reached out to me to learn about my career path. The idea of being a coach continued to resurface.

In February 2011, I found myself making a last-minute trip to the Nordstrom's shoe department in Seattle, Washington, while I was visiting my brother. As I tried on variations of bridesmaid shoes, I overheard another woman (Nancy) who was trying on shoes nearby mention that she was a coach. My ears immediately perked up, and I wanted to know more.

A number of questions came to mind:

- What kind of coach are you?
- How did you get into coaching?
- Did you go through a training program?
- What type of work do you do?
- Do you have your own coaching business?

I asked her one question, "Where did you do your coach training?" And just like that Nancy and I fell deep into conversation about the world of coach training programs and the process of becoming a coach. I found out that she had attended the Hudson Institute of Coaching, a well-respected coach training program primarily focused on executive and transition coaching. The Hudson Institute of Coaching happened to be where my dad's coach had done his training.

> *The world of coaching spoke to me, and I was excited about using coaching as a tool to impact individuals more directly.*

I had already spoken with Toni McLean, COO of the Hudson Institute of Coaching, several months earlier about whether Hudson might be a good fit for me as I started researching coach training programs. I recognized that coaching skills could help me progress in my career and move me closer to what was next—even though I wasn't completely sure what that was. I also wanted to take the time and space to think about my personal and professional goals. The world of coaching spoke to me, and I was excited about using coaching as a tool to impact individuals more directly. Running into Nancy at Nordstrom reignited my interest in coaching, and I resolved to consider it more seriously.

I decided to attend LifeLaunch, a three-day workshop offered by the Hudson Institute, as well as a one-day introduction-to-coaching workshop. I loved the exercises at Hudson, and I bonded with the people in my group. Later, I even hired one of the attendees to be my coach. Santa Barbara, where Hudson is based, felt like the perfect backdrop (ocean and mountains) to think about myself and develop my coaching skills. I walked away from the workshop surprised and intrigued to learn about how coaching is actually delivered to clients, and I was curious to learn more.

When I returned from LifeLaunch, I had the opportunity to become a certified coach within the company where I worked.

I learned more about coaching in an organizational setting, and I was able to coach both internal employees and external clients. While I gained firsthand experience coaching in my company, I knew I wanted to go through a more formal program outside of the company to gain even more confidence in my coaching skills and abilities.

In addition to Hudson, I was also considering Georgetown's Certificate in Leadership Coaching Program, which is based in Washington, DC, where I live. I researched the program, talked to several Georgetown coaching graduates to learn more, and observed a coach who had graduated from the program as she facilitated a workshop in the community.

I was conflicted about my options: Did it make sense to attend a program that would help me work with aspiring leaders within my company and community? Should I pursue other trainings that would immerse me in nature and connect me to the earth and environment? I knew that I wanted a program that would catapult me professionally, and it came down to a decision between Hudson and Georgetown. I didn't even look into other programs at the time since they weren't on my radar. In retrospect, I'm amazed at the programs that could have catered to my "Mama Earth" side.

After much deliberation, I selected Georgetown's program because it would help me build my network of coaches locally in DC. Its focus on leaders within organizations catered to my interest in leadership and systems thinking. The university affiliation would provide me with an academic learning environment conducive to testing ideas. I also liked the balance of theory and application.

Having completed the Georgetown program, I have since decided to leave my job and embark on a new direction in my career. I have too many interests and too much curiosity to commit to being a full-time coach; so while I do coach individuals, I prefer to blend coaching skills into the consulting, training, and facilitation work that I do. I like the problem-solving aspect of consulting, the educational component of training, the collaborative nature of facilitation, and the presence-based aspect of coaching.

You might be wondering what my definition of coaching is. I see coaching as a powerful communication tool—one that can transform individuals and communities. I see the principles of coaching—connectedness, attunement, and self-inquiry—as tools that have the power to ignite social change.

Tactically speaking, coaching involves two parties: the coach and the client. The coach is a trusting, invested individual who provides a confidential and comfortable space for a coaching relationship to exist and will use presence, listening skills, and powerful questions to support the client's intended outcomes. The client is resourceful and willing to engage in self-reflection and discovery. This is my current working definition, and I look forward to further honing it as I evolve in my career.

My exposure to coaching has opened up a whole new world of opportunity, both personally and professionally. In fact, writing this book has been another way for me to explore my interest in the coaching world. My coaching journey has already taught me a lot, and it's only just begun.

For more information on this book and other resources for coaches, please visit **www.coachingiscalling.com**.

INTRODUCTION

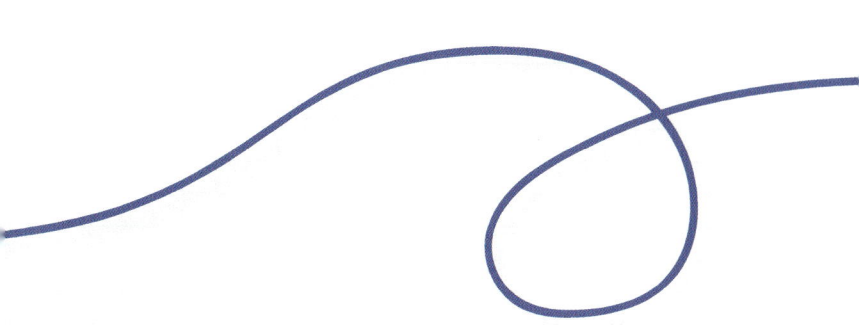

WHY I WROTE THIS BOOK

When I decided to pursue coaching and began researching coach training programs, I came across dozens of websites, articles, and online posts about coaching. I was overwhelmed by the deluge of information and had a difficult time discerning between what was a valid or reputable program and what was just noise.

Each program's website was filled with great content, but I kept looking (unsuccessfully) for the equivalent of a *US News & World Report* ranking of coach training programs. Where was the guide that would tell me everything I needed to know about coach training?

Even after I selected a coach training program and completed it, I was still drawn to the idea of researching coach training programs and interviewing coaches in order to write a comprehensive guide to coach training programs. Through my research and interviews, I realized that a framework to help people understand the world of coaching and professional career paths would also be helpful.

In writing this book, my goal is to help you navigate the world of coaching with reliable information so you can make the best decision for how to move forward with coaching.

The questions I had when I started my coaching research are the same ones that I address in this guide:

- What is coaching, and what do I need to know about coaching?
- What are the first steps I should take if I want to become a coach?
- What do I need to know about coach training programs?
- How do I select the right coach training program for me?
- What resources do I need to know about as a new coach?

If you are reading this book, my hope is that you are interested in a coaching career path and are considering your next move.

HOW TO READ THIS BOOK

I have approached this book in coachlike fashion. There are worksheets and questions for you to reflect on as you read through the content. Take the time to answer the questions, which will support you in selecting a coach training program if you decide that is the right choice for you. The worksheets and the Pause reflections are an introduction into the process you will encounter as a coach.

As you embark on this coaching journey, consider the following:

- What type of coaching do I want to do?
- What kind of clients do I want to serve?

These two questions will be explored throughout this book, and the worksheets and Pause reflections will help you to better answer them. You might want to consider keeping a journal while you answer these questions. I have also included extra pages in the back of the book.

The book is organized into five sections:

- **Part I:** Your Coaching Journey
- **Part II:** What You Need to Know about Coaching
- **Part III:** What You Need to Know about Coach Training Programs
- **Part IV:** Find the Coach Training Program That Best Fits Your Needs
- **Part V:** Coaching Resources

In Part I, I ask you to think about your personal interests and experiences that will inform you as a coach. I also share my thoughts on how to think about your coaching journey.

In Part II, I discuss what coaching is and present a way of thinking about coaching. I also expand on the professional opportunities and coaching career paths that exist. I briefly discuss related fields and prompt you to think about the clients you may want to work with.

In Part III, I describe the benefits of coach training programs. I also elaborate on the investment you will make in your training and the logistical considerations, and I offer questions for reflection.

Part IV will help you to identify the coach training program that best fits your needs. There is a comprehensive worksheet that lists considerations for coach training programs with questions to support self-discovery and research.

Part V includes resources that will help you to jump-start your coaching career. These resources range from associations to coaching magazines and everything in between. In this part of the book, I share tactical ways that you can take immediate action to maximize these resources.

METHODOLOGY

Over the course of ten months, I interviewed more than forty people in the coaching field. I selected fifteen coaching certification programs (which I refer to as coach training programs) that offer a range of experiences, including many of the better-known programs in North America. I interviewed administrators and graduates from these programs to support my own research. You can view a list of these programs in the Resources section.

I also interviewed select experts in the coaching field to understand their perspectives and the advice they have for new coaches. I scoured LinkedIn coaching message boards to better understand the conversations taking place in the coaching world around issues such as certification and accreditation, and surveyed a group of coaches to solicit input on training and personal development.

A WORD BEFORE YOU BEGIN

I have focused on explaining the world of coaching in this book, rather than how to actually coach. Most of what I've written applies to one-on-one coaching, though I have included references to team coaching, or group coaching, when possible. Though this book is focused on North America, I have also incorporated perspectives from the international coaching scene when applicable. It is my hope that this book will help you think about your coaching journey, what's important to you as a coach, and what training is the best fit for you.

I believe that coaching is a powerful tool for both individuals and organizations, and the journey of becoming a coach is fruitful and full of insight and discovery. Coaching will change you and the way you interact with the world. Get excited!

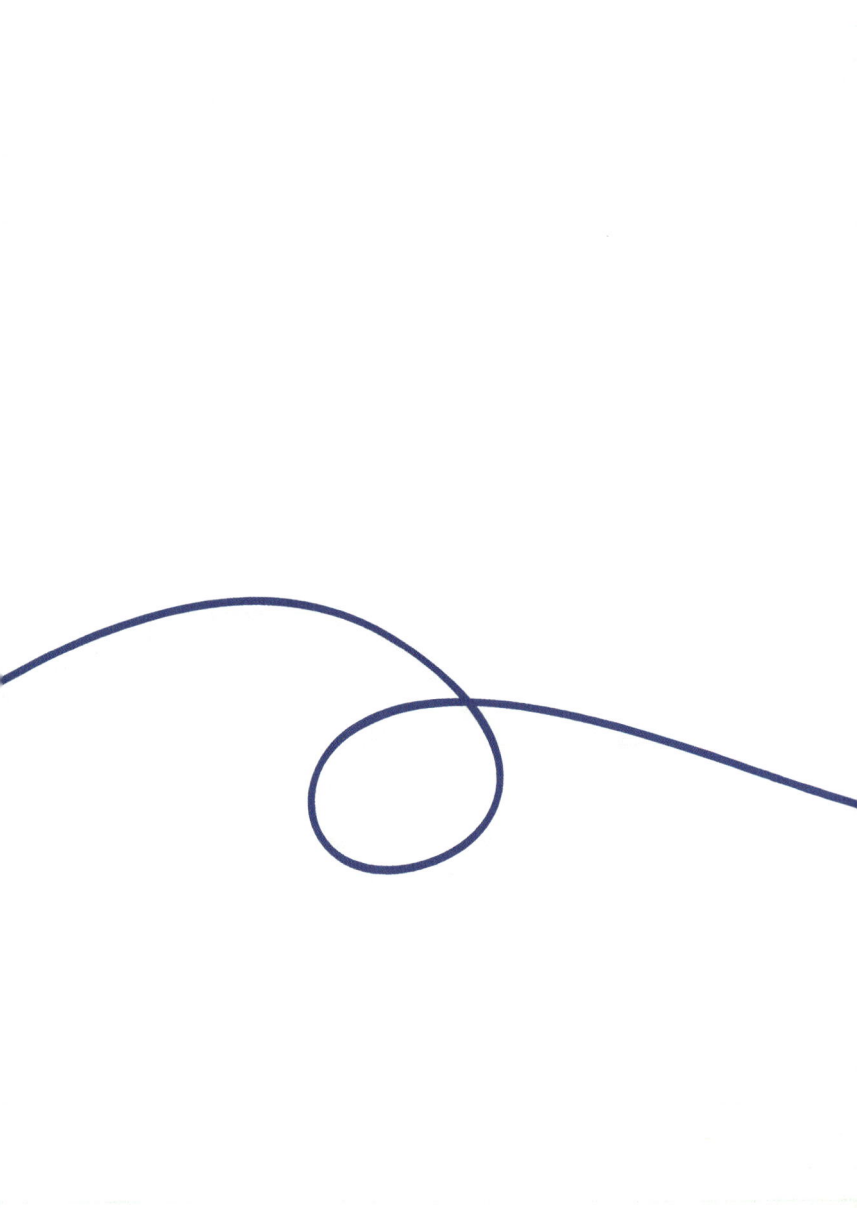

PART I
YOUR COACHING JOURNEY

WORKSHEET:
WHY COACHING? WHY NOW?

Coaching might feel like the word that best describes the work you're doing or are interested in doing. But is it really coaching that you want to do? What is drawing you to coaching right now?

Do you…

- Already coach and want to formalize your training?
- Feel that coaching skills would enhance your current skill set?
- Keep hearing from peers and friends that you would make a good coach, and want to investigate further?
- Think that others can benefit from your experience and role as a trusted advisor?
- Want to embark on a new professional direction?
- Work with a coach and think, "I want to have that job!"
- Want to know what all the coaching fuss is about?

Do you just have an inkling that you want to be a coach?

Before I share my research and analysis on the coaching profession and how you can start to think about coach training programs, it will be helpful for you to understand what's drawing you to coaching.

Take a few moments to sit and reflect on your reasons for wanting to pursue coaching. You might want to turn off your phone, computer, and other technology and find a place where you will not be distracted. Write down your initial thoughts on why coaching appeals to you and why now might be the time to pursue your interest in coaching. You can use the questions below as a guide.

Why Coaching?

Why do you want to be a coach?

_____
_____
_____

What has prepared you for a career in coaching up until now? Think about your personal story and the experiences you have had both inside and outside of work.

_____
_____
_____

Why Now?

What is drawing you to coaching right now?

_____
_____
_____

What do you hope coaching will open up for you?

_____
_____
_____

What More?

What unanswered questions do you have about coaching?

_____
_____
_____

What do you need to make a decision about coaching?

_____
_____
_____

Keep your answers in mind as you go through this book. Remember to compare what you learn about coach training programs with your own motivations for coaching and then use that information to decide what the best path is for you.

> **❝** *Bill George, in his book* True North, *talks about 'crucible moments'—a time in your life where you hit a particular situation and you ask yourself larger life questions like 'Is there more?' That happened to me in my early forties, and that's when I decided that a common theme in my life had been coaching and creativity in teams, and it led me to where I am today."*

—Deb St. John, executive coach, strategist, and training professional (certified somatic coach from Strozzi Institute and certificate in leadership coaching from Georgetown University)

PART I

There are different paths to coaching, yet in many interviews and conversations I heard common themes around struggle, breakdown, and breakthrough and the reward that coaching has brought to people's lives.

In Joseph Campbell's *The Hero with a Thousand Faces*, he addresses mythological heroes who are called to action and must overcome various obstacles before they can claim victory. To extend this idea to your own journey, ask yourself: *What is my story, and how does coaching fit in?*

For you, there may have been a call to coaching that showed up in a conversation with a coworker or friend, a chance meeting at a local coffee shop, or a deliberate discussion with a coach. There might have been a refusal or a hesitancy to move forward with making a change in your life until a mentor or friend encouraged you and even supported you. There is self-reflection along with deliberate steps that you take as you progress in the path that you are defining. It is the journey itself that is rewarding, and along the way, there are certain hurdles you overcome to get there.

In this section, I focus on the common steps or actions that will be part of your coaching journey. At the heart of it is exploring yourself and your interests and understanding how coaching fits into your narrative. How are you the hero in your own journey?

DO THE WORK ON YOURSELF

As part of the process of becoming a coach, you will need to work on yourself so that you understand where you are coming from and what your blind spots are. What do I mean by "work on yourself"? *Know thyself*. Know who you are, what you stand for, and how your personality shows up in your relationships and interactions. Your own capacity to know yourself will support your ability to help others to know themselves.

For example, if you are coaching someone who is expressing angst about finding a new job and it's a topic that's bothering you, you might find yourself triggered into thinking about yourself and your employment history instead of the client. As a coach, you have to be mentally, emotionally, and physically prepared to support your client.

Pamela McLean, in *The Completely Revised Handbook of Coaching*, refers to this concept as "self as coach." It is at the center of her recommendation for masterful coaching and the primary starting point for becoming a coach. She talks about a coach's "inner landscape: habits and behaviors, long-held stories, and our ways of making meaning and living in the world." This is the challenging and exciting work of becoming a coach. It is also a lifelong practice.

McLean offers a framework for thinking about "self as coach" across six domains: presence, empathetic stance, range of feelings, boundary awareness, somatic awareness, and courage to challenge. These topics are a way for you think about what it means to work on "self as coach" and start to gain awareness around the domain you're in with yourself and ultimately where you will be with your client at a given time. Her book further expands on practices and resources to support coaches in these domains.

Below I have offered questions to guide you in thinking about "self as coach" and how you view and interact with the world.

Take a deep breath in and exhale out. By taking a pause, you can start to notice what's going on around you and what you're experiencing. Notice what you see, what you smell, what you hear, and what you taste. Notice the touch of the paper or electronic reader. Try to stay in the present as you answer these questions as best as you can.

What are your values? What is important to you?

_____

_____

_____

What gives you meaning?

_____

_____

_____

Your Coaching Journey

What energizes you?

What exhausts you?

What relaxes you?

How are you achieving the outcomes you want in life?

What experiences inform your viewpoint?

How do people respond to you?

What would others say are your strengths and weaknesses?

___

Now take the time to reflect on your responses. How do you know this information? What patterns do you see? What have you learned about yourself already? Write down any observations and insights you have had as you've thought about yourself.

___

Even as you work through the questions above, the process of self-reflection and "self as coach" does not stop. As you become a coach, it's important for you to be hyperaware of your own ways of viewing the world. You will be modeling the very principles that you will work on with your clients.

CREATE YOUR OWN DEVELOPMENTAL PATH

As you explore coaching, there will be hundreds of resources and trainings available to you. Learning is a huge part of becoming a coach, and you will be introduced to new concepts and ideas in coaching. Perhaps you already have an inclination about what subjects interest you. Coaching may even trigger ideas you've always been interested in.

It will be helpful for you to identify what you need and want to know as you construct your own developmental path. What you choose to learn about might satisfy your own curiosity. It may also be applicable to your clients who are looking to you for both your knowledge and expertise as a coach.

Robert Thomas, in *Crucibles of Leadership*, discusses the importance of crucible moments—key experiences that shape you as a leader. He talks about these moments as an opportunity to discover how you learn and how you lead. He suggests that leaders create a personal learning strategy to maximize crucible experiences and to learn from them.

As you become a coach, I think a similar process applies. Think about how you learn and what key experiences you have had (or are going to have) that inform how you coach. Creating a developmental path, or plan, is one step you can take to map out what and how you want to learn.

DIAGRAM 1: Example Developmental Plan

Short Term (6 months to 12 months)

Learning Opportunity	Timeframe	Learning Topic	Learning Objective
Introduction to Coaching Workshop	Summer 2014	Coaching Skills	Understand basic principles of coaching
Coaching Certification Program	Enrolled by September 2014	General Certification	Work with individual clients and in teams

Medium Term (1 to 3 years)

Learning Opportunity	Timeframe	Learning Topic	Learning Objective
Team Coaching Training	December 2015	Specialized Training in Team Coaching	Learn team dynamics and coaching techniques to bring to consulting and coaching
Drawing on the Right Side of the Brain	March 2016	Creativity and Innovation	Self-development and creative thinking

Long Term (3 to 5 years)

Learning Opportunity	Timeframe	Learning Topic	Learning Objective
Master's or PhD Program, Organizational Development or I-O Psychology	Enrolled by 2018	Team Dynamics	Consulting at Executive level; Become thought leader and publish articles

Take a few minutes to reflect on what topics interest you that may or may not be directly related to coaching. You may be interested in adult development, team dynamics, and/or Gestalt theory. You may also be interested in other subjects such as storytelling, improvisation theater, and graphic arts. Think about how these topics of interest can help you better yourself and how they might support your coaching. Write your thoughts down or draw a visual to capture these interests. You can then start to incorporate these ideas into a plan.

Assuming coaching is part of this picture, there are dozens of free webinars, articles, and blogs that can introduce you to coaching, several of which are listed in Part V. You can buy books or download YouTube videos to help you learn to coach and try on coaching yourself.

Coach training programs are one way to start gathering the skills and practice to support your coaching journey. Going through a coach training program doesn't ensure that you will be a masterful coach when you complete the program. It is just one part of your learning path.

You might also want to consider hiring a coach to experience coaching firsthand. You can only speculate so much on the benefits of coaching. Having a coach helps you discern the difference between what coaching is and what it isn't (assuming you end up with a good coach!). You will not only be able to work on yourself, but will also learn tools and techniques that can inform how you want to coach others. It's a never-ending giving cycle.

> *I read every day: articles, blogs, and books. I listen to tapes/CDs and TED talks, watch videos, and take professional development classes. Getting paid when you coach is one issue, but keeping up with hours of study with no financial reward is the investment I gratefully pay to be professional."*

—Judy Krings, PhD, personal and professional positive psychology strengths and well-being coach (certified MentorCoach)

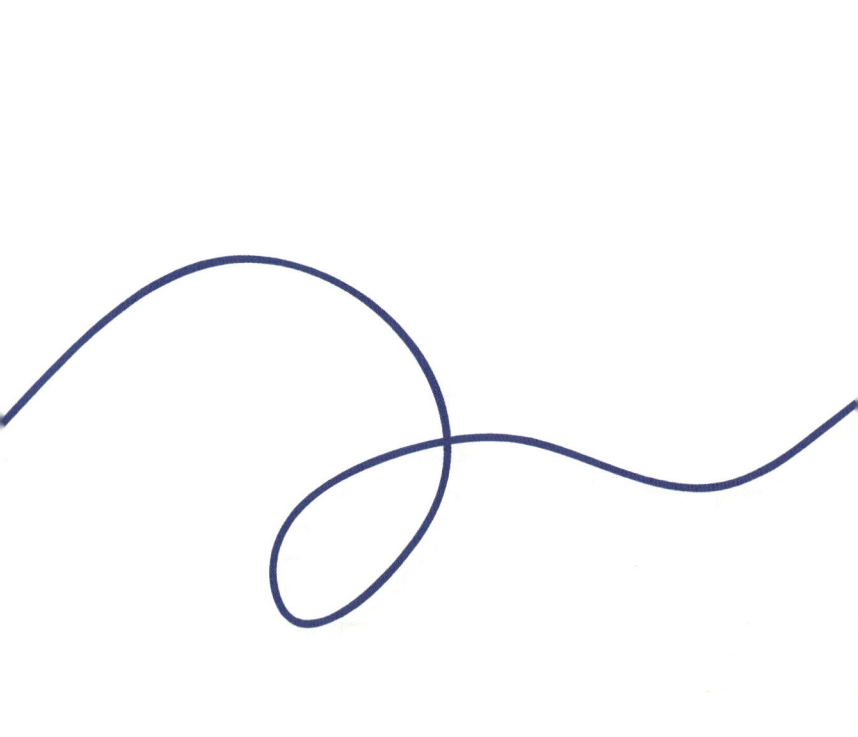

PART II
WHAT YOU NEED TO KNOW ABOUT COACHING

PART II

Coaching emerged from philosophy and the social sciences, and it draws on a variety of disciplines. Dr. Vikki Brock does an excellent job of describing the roots and profession of coaching in her book Sourcebook of Coaching History *in which you can learn about the history of coaching and how it has evolved.*

According to Dr. Brock, the most influential fields that have impacted coaching are philosophy, business (in the areas of management, consulting, organizational development, human resources, training), psychology, sports (athletics, fitness, and recreation), human potential movement, and education. These disciplines inform the approach you will use as a coach. They also influence the way that coach training programs teach coaching.

In this section, I describe coaching in simple terms. I detail what the coach and client interaction looks like and explore the intersection between what the client needs and what the coach offers. I provide a framework in which you can understand how to think about coaching and what types of coaches exist, from the client's perspective. I also address the coach's point of view by discussing professional opportunities in coaching and fields related to coaching. I end this section with a worksheet that you can use to determine what type of clients you want to work with and where you fit in.

COACHING 101

Before we explore the client and coach interaction, I want to state a basic principle that is at the heart of coaching: coach and client are both resourceful. In coaching, it is assumed that clients have the answers, and as a coach you are able to help them see their thinking and actions more clearly. You will help clients understand their opportunities and challenges in new or different ways. You will draw on your resourcefulness and creativity to customize a unique and individualized approach for each of your clients.

DIAGRAM 2: Coach and Client Sweet Spot

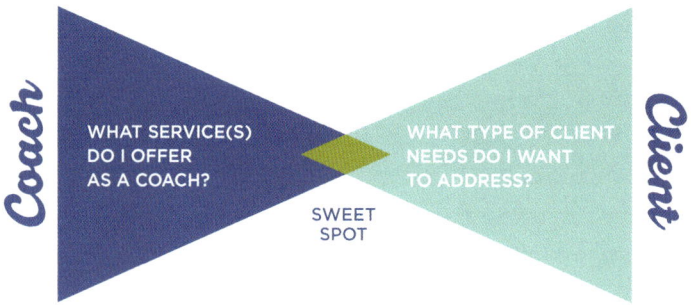

CLIENTS HAVE A NEED

Clients often have a need or a desired outcome that they want to work on such as "achieving work-life balance" or "speaking up in meetings" or "working on interpersonal relationships." They might be looking for a coach who can help them work through whatever issue or challenge they are facing. They might come to you as a self-described "working mom" or "overworked manager" based on the roles they play and the responsibilities they have. Or they might come to you with specific needs based on their current stage in life. People hire coaches for various reasons and at different points in their lives.

COACHES OFFER A SERVICE

As a coach, you will provide a safe space for your clients to feel heard, and you will actively listen to and question your clients to help them find ways of working through their challenges. Your role will be to pay attention to the language, body, and emotion that the client presents and enable your client to help shift behavior and ultimately achieve the outcome she or he desires.

The sweet spot is where you offer a service that addresses the client's need. Your ability to connect with the client and also your shared interest will help to build the connection. From this point you can decide how you are going to structure your coaching engagements and what tools, frameworks, and resources you will use to support you in your coaching.

> *The sweet spot is where you offer a service that addresses the client's need.*

In the future, you may consider developing a niche target client demographic to differentiate yourself as a coach, and you may offer other services in addition to coaching. Many coaches wear different hats, serving as facilitators, trainers, educators, and more.

What You Need to Know about Coaching

The need to offer diversified services is also driven by what the client asks for. If you are coaching within an organization, does the client really want to hire a coach, a strategic advisor, and a leadership development expert? They might come to you with all three requests.

DIAGRAM 3: Coach Response to Different Clients

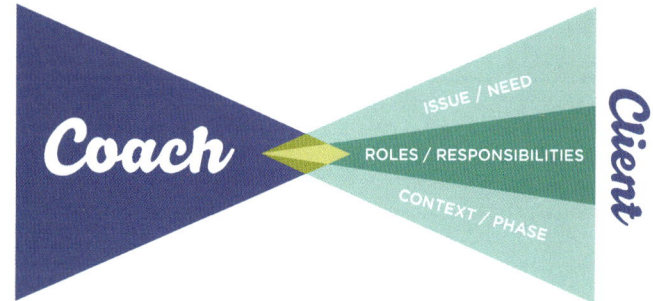

HOW TO THINK ABOUT COACHING

When it comes to deciding what type of coach you want to be, it's really about the client you want to serve. When asked what makes a good coach, many coaches suggest that it's in the eye of the beholder—namely, the client. Good reviews and outcomes from clients and organizations that you work with will drive business. Keeping the client in mind, it's helpful to start thinking about where you fit and how you will know if the work you're doing is successful. If you're wondering, coaching is measured in return on investment or return on engagement just like other business endeavors.

Clients typically won't know that they want to focus on "appreciative inquiry" or "emotional intelligence" even though as a coach you may have this knowledge. Your clients will most likely think about working with a coach when issues come up that they are stuck on, such as managing teams or maintaining a healthy lifestyle while constantly traveling for work. The client might need support in connection to the role or responsibilities that come with being an executive director or partner. At the same time, the client might be dealing with change and adversity based on a phase in his or her life, such as finding a new job or taking care of elderly parents.

In the following section, I expand on these different ways of looking at coaching and highlight the types of coaches that respond to these needs.

As you read through the information below, think about what types of coaching match your interests.

Pay attention to that voice in your head that shouts, "Yes!"—or that gut feeling that makes you cringe as you read the descriptions. You may want to consider making two lists—a "yes" list (where you can see yourself coaching) and a "no" list (where you don't see yourself coaching)—as you start to think about what clients you want to serve.

Write down any initial thoughts about what type of coaching interests you.

_____
_____
_____

RESPONDING TO CLIENTS' ISSUES OR IMMEDIATE NEEDS

The client brings a specific issue or immediate need to the coaching engagement though this might not necessarily be what's actually at the core of the problem. This is the first way the client is able to identify that something is not working. The issue could range from dealing with the loss of someone close who has passed away to addressing challenges in health (or feeling like so much change is happening at the same time).

Depending on how your clients understand coaching, they might start their search by looking for a coach who addresses their needs. The client who says "I want to figure out what do with my life" might be inclined to look for a life coach. Someone who wants to change careers might look for a career coach. Someone who is dealing with relationship challenges might look for a coach who specializes in relationships.

Below are some examples of coaches who may focus on specific issues.

- **Relationship Coach:** focus on interpersonal dynamics and emotional well-being (also: dating coach)

- **Health and Wellness Coach:** focus on health, fitness, nutrition, mental health, and well-being (also: health coach, nutrition coach, weight-loss coach)
- **Grief Coach:** focus on dealing with loss

Other types of coaches include **attention deficit disorder (ADD)** coaches, who help clients manage the symptoms of ADD; **personal brand coaches**, who help clients identify and convey what services they offer, and even **book coaches**, who help writers conceptualize or complete book projects.

Some of the coaches address very specific client needs. It can be helpful for people seeking coaches to find coaches who have the very title and service offering they're looking for. At the same time, the extensive number of coaching titles that exist can be confusing. Some of the naming options exist purely for marketing purposes, and the variety of naming conventions could be attributed to semantics.

Note: *You can pick your own title as a coach; this means that you can decide the name that works best for you and will attract the clients you're looking for. Your only limitation is your imagination.*

RESPONDING TO CLIENTS' ROLES AND RESPONSIBILITIES

Another way to think about coaching is to consider the roles and responsibilities clients bring with them. The client could be an entrepreneur working in a fast-paced, undefined work environment, a manager responsible for leading teams, or an executive setting the strategic direction of her organization.

The coaches listed below focus on the roles and responsibilities of their clients:

- **Executive Coach:** focus on C-suite or senior leaders within organizations, working on strategy and visioning, succession planning, and leadership
- **Leadership Coach:** focus on individuals in leadership roles, especially those in positions of (new) authority and responsible for delegation and motivating team members
- **Parenting Coach:** focus on providing support to parents balancing the demands of family or working with challenging children

A 2009 *Harvard Business Review* article entitled "What Can Coaches Do For You?" found that there has been a shift in recent years within organizations—away from programs that use coaching to correct behavior and toward coaching as a perk for high-performing leaders. While companies hire coaches to support high performers improve in their professional roles, personal issues are often discussed with these executives. Other coaches who respond to the roles and responsibilities of clients might specialize in working with nonprofit leaders, for example.

RESPONDING TO CONTEXTS OR PHASES OF CLIENTS' LIVES

You can also approach coaching more generally, by context or phase. Context refers to how your clients are living their lives and where they may be working. Phase refers to what they are going through in life, such as making a transition, dealing with a midlife or quarter-life crisis, or changing careers.

The coaches listed below focus on the context or phase their clients are in:

- **Life Coach:** focus on supporting individuals considering both professional and personal dimensions of life (also: **personal coach** and **professional coach**)
- **Career Coach:** focus on supporting individuals shifting careers and making decisions about next steps (also: **transitional coach**); may focus on quarter-life crisis, midlife crisis, or creating a legacy
- **Business Coach:** focus on an individual working within an organizational context (also: **organizational coach** and **corporate coach**); related to executive coach and leadership coach but often more general

These coaches may do the exact same coaching as the ones who focus on issues or on roles and responsibilities. However, these coaches might prefer to address a broader range of issues and have a "generalist" title, often because this better reflects the type of coaching they do and the clients they intend to serve.

Even within these ways of thinking about coaching, there are subspecialties within and across these three categories. For example, there are career coaches that focus on MBA applicants and others that focus on careers in social impact.

WORKSHEET:
WHAT KIND OF CLIENTS DO YOU WANT TO SERVE?

Think about the reaction you had to the types of coaches you just read through. What resonated with you? What type of coaching and coaches did you identify with, and which descriptions had you running the other way? Refer back to any notes you took. Take the time that you need to reflect on the questions below and answer them as best as you can.

Think about what <u>issues and challenges</u> you might like to focus on.

What topics are you passionate about? How could this translate into specific issues or challenges your target clients might have?

_____
_____
_____

If you're attending a dinner party, what conversations are you usually drawn to? Are there certain topics that consistently show up for you?

___

Examples:
- *Everyone knows that you are the go-to person for advice on a particular topic (e.g., the latest technology, financial investing, or starting a new business).*
- *Your friends always call you when they are having relationship problems.*

Think about <u>what types of people</u> you would like to support.

How would you describe the people you like working with? What roles and responsibilities do they have?

___

Do you want to work with individuals, teams, and/or organizations?

___

Examples:
- *The high performers in your organization reach out to you to learn how they can get promoted to the next level.*
- *You are often called in by leadership teams to problem solve and negotiate challenging work situations.*

Think about what <u>life stage or context</u> you would like to support.

What transformational or "crucible" experiences have led you to where you are?

_____
_____
_____

Examples:
- *Your friends or colleagues often come to you when they are changing jobs, and they ask you review their resumes.*
- *Your friends or colleagues frequently seek your advice on all types of problems they are having.*

Write down any insights you have had about yourself and your thoughts about the client demographic you're interested in serving.

_____
_____
_____

PROFESSIONAL OPPORTUNITIES AND CAREER PATHS

Based on who you want to coach and what topics most interest you, you have a number of professional options. As a consideration, the amount of money you will charge for your services will depend on the clients you serve, your personal value, and what path you decide to pursue. It will also depend on whether you can earn an income purely from coaching.

I have listed a number of commonly pursued career paths for professional coaches, which I expand on below.

- Internally, or inside organizations in a coaching capacity
- Independently, or contracting to individuals and organizations
- Formal collaboration with a firm specializing in coaching
- Formal or informal collaboration with other coaches

Please note that these are not mutually exclusive, as you may work for yourself, contract with organizations, and also collaborate with other coaches. However, this is a way for you to start thinking about what your options are and how you are going to integrate your work as a coach with what you're doing now.

Internally, or inside organizations in a coaching capacity

If you already work in an organization or want to be gainfully employed by an organization, this is a commonly pursued option. Depending on how advanced the leadership and coaching space is within your organization, you might be forging new territory and creating a position for yourself. You might be able to work within the existing context of learning, training, and/or leadership. You might also decide to bring your coaching expertise into your current work.

Note: *A trend in the corporate and to a lesser degree the nonprofit world has been to grow a cadre of internal coaches which is often more cost effective than contracting externally. Some organizations offer internal coach training programs and supplementary coaching skill training to support their managers and leaders.*

Independently, or contracting to individuals and organizations

This is an alternative option to working within an organization. If you are contracting to individuals and organizations, you have more flexibility in choosing your own work but potentially less stability in having a steady employer. Individual clients may reach out to you directly through referrals. RFPs (requests for proposals) may be sent to you through your formal and informal networks seeking individual coaches or groups of coaches.

Some of the RFPs require coaches to have experience with specific tools and assessments such as Myers-Briggs Type Indicator (MBTI) or 360-degree assessments.

Note: *Being a great coach and being an entrepreneur are different skill sets and you may have to leave your comfort zone to network with people and organizations for clients. If you have the appetite to promote yourself and find your* *own clients, then this could be a great opportunity for you. There are online tools and websites to help you advertise your services.*

Formal collaboration with a firm specializing in coaching

Some firms specialize in coaching and enable you to have a career in coaching along with the stability of working for an organization. These firms may offer a range of related services, such as leadership development, organizational effectiveness, employee engagement, change management, workforce transitions, and more. You may be required to follow their coaching protocol/system.

Note: *For reference, you can look into organizations such as Personnel Decisions International (PDI Ninth House), Hay Group, Aon Corporation, Towers Watson HR Consulting, Lee Hecht Harrison, Right Management, and CoachSource.*

As you get into coaching, you will form your own distinctions about these professions. You might also be able to tap into trainings, networking groups, and conferences that these related professions offer. Many of these related fields have their own associations that you can join. You might even realize that coaching is a gateway to other professional opportunities that appeal to you.

Formal or informal collaboration with other coaches

Coaches commonly refer clients and other coaches to one another and are constantly exploring ways of working together to maximize their resources. Many coaches informally partner together to deliver workshops or programs, sometimes in response to RFPs. Some coaches formally create their own business entity and have associate coaches work with them. Another emerging trend is licensing of coaches' intellectual property that other coaches can use for a cost.

Note: *Relax. You don't need to decide right now where or how you will set up your work. This is just the start of thinking about where and how you see yourself working. It's also meant to get you thinking about the financial implications of coaching.*

RELATED FIELDS TO CONSIDER

It is helpful to understand where your interests as a coach may overlap with other professions. As you read about the categories discussed above, you might have thought, "What's the line between coaching and therapy . . . or coaching and management training?" There is certainly overlap with related professions, which include psychology, counseling, training and development, and industrial-organizational psychology, to name a few.

As you get into coaching, you will form your own distinctions about these professions. You might also be able to tap into trainings, networking groups, and conferences that these related professions offer. Many of these related fields have their own associations that you can join. You might even realize that coaching is a gateway to other professional opportunities that appeal to you.

Think about the work you've done so far to identify the type of coaching that you are interested in. What do you plan to do with your coaching? Do you plan to coach full-time and create a sustainable lifestyle for yourself? Do you plan to learn coaching skills so that you can incorporate them into a job? Do you want to dabble in coaching because it makes you feel good?

Write down what you plan to do with your coaching, referencing the questions above.

_____
_____
_____

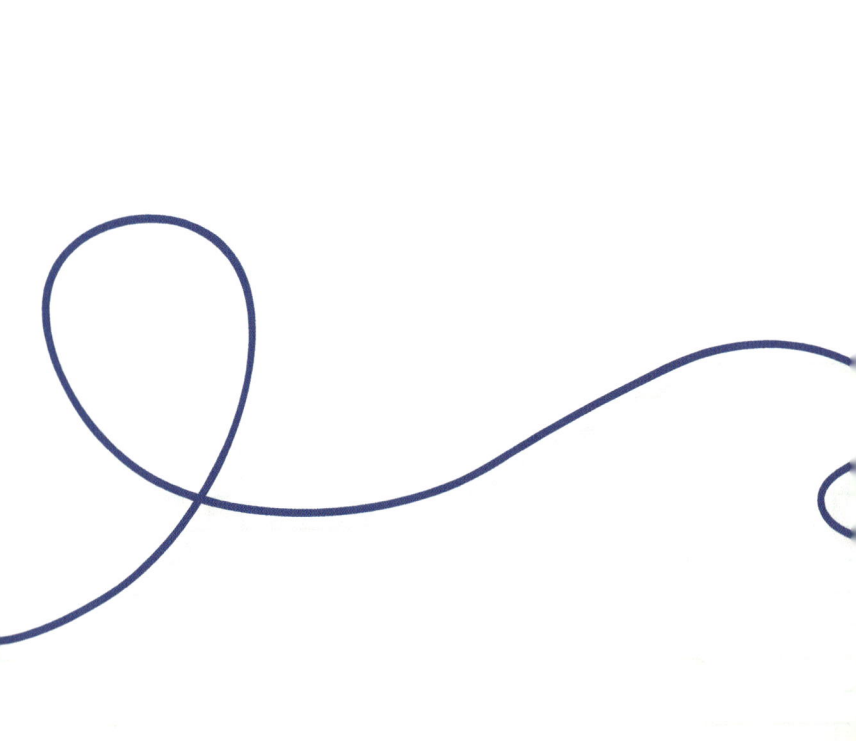

PART III
WHAT YOU NEED TO KNOW ABOUT COACH TRAINING PROGRAMS

In this section, I share multiple ways to think about the value or benefits of a coach training program. Based on my research and interviews, I highlight common themes that run across programs and share relevant examples. I also discuss program logistics and the investment that coach training programs require.

Many coach training programs share the same underpinnings—the basic building blocks for coaching skills and ways of working on your own personal development. At a minimum, coach training programs will provide you with the basic skills of coaching such as active listening and powerful questions. While the programs' philosophies and curricula vary widely, programs that are accredited by the same associations often follow similar standards. For example, as part of your training, you might be required to submit recorded coaching sessions and receive feedback on your coaching based on where the program is accredited; there might also be a final oral and written exam and a capstone project.

In this guide, I have focused on programs that offer some form of certification and certificate option. There are an abundance of shorter, more focused trainings and non-certification options, which I have not included, as there are too many to list and they are often more targeted at specific learning topics.

DIAGRAM 4: Coach Training Program Building Blocks

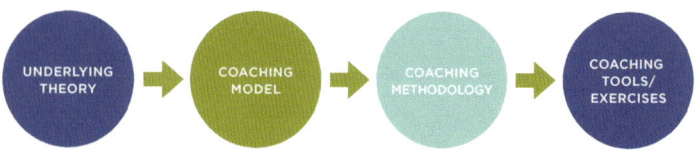

Programs may include some or all of the following:

- **Underlying Theory:** the context from root disciplines that inform and influence coaching (may also include evidence-based or researched findings to support coaching)
- **Coaching Model:** the high-level strategy/framework that creates a structure for thinking about your coaching sessions
- **Coaching Methodology:** the process that you will take with your clients from start to finish in each of your coaching sessions
- **Coaching Tools/Exercises:** the supporting material that you can use when working with clients (may also be referred to as practices, templates, or workbooks)

BENEFITS OF A COACH TRAINING PROGRAM

In today's marketplace, you can call yourself a coach—and you are magically a coach! However, as the field of coaching evolves, more individuals and organizations are asking about professional training and credentials. Credentials are more or less important depending on the type of coach you want to be and the market you want to serve. You will want to keep this in mind as you think about how to position yourself.

The coaches who decide not to attend coach training programs don't see the relevance or importance. They may have years of experience in related industries. Also, because many clients don't ask for credentials and some of the best coaches are self-taught, they don't think it's necessary to do coach training. However, coach training programs are a great way to jump-start your coaching career. As you will soon see, training programs will benefit you in other ways as well.

DIAGRAM 5: Six Key Benefits of Coach Training Programs

1. COACHING CERTIFICATION AND REPUTATION	2. DIFFERENT APPROACHES TO COACHING	3. ACCESS TO COACHING COLLEAGUES
4. A CONTINUOUS LEARNING ENVIRONMENT	5. FOCUS ON DEVELOPING YOURSELF	6. SUPPORT TO LAUNCH A COACHING BUSINESS

1. Coaching Certification and Reputation: You will receive a certification or credential that is respected in the marketplace and gain access to any affiliations the program may have.

2. Different Approaches to Coaching: You will gain access to models, methodologies, frameworks, tools, and practices as well as exposure to the related theories to support your coaching practice.

3. Access to Coaching Colleagues: You will deepen your interpersonal connections to the coaching community through interactions with your faculty/instructors, peers, and the alumni network.

4. A Continuous Learning Environment: You will have opportunities to practice and hone your skills and take your learning to higher levels.

5. Focus on Developing Yourself: You will have the time and space to focus on your own personal development and receive coaching and mentorship.

6. Support to Define Your Coaching Package: You may reflect on what your personal brand is and how to build your own coaching practice.

COACHING CERTIFICATION AND REPUTATION

1. COACHING CERTIFICATION AND REPUTATION

It's often difficult to know what a coach training program's reputation or ranking is. Some programs claim to be "the Harvard of coaching" or the "top program," but there's really no objective source awarding these titles. Coaching is an emerging profession, and the nascent coaching community has not unanimously agreed on standards and coaching competencies. Word of mouth is often the social currency of reputation.

When it comes to gauging a program's reputation, you can pay attention to several factors. You can look at how long the program has been in existence and whether it is affiliated with any coaching associations. You can look at who is running the program, and his or her background, experience, and reputation in the coaching industry (Has this person been published? Is he or she still involved?). Lastly, you can learn about what graduates of the program have gone on to after graduating.

Some clients won't ask about your coaching credential. Others will want to know more about your background and training. They will likely want to have a phone conversation or in-person meeting to learn about what you offer. Corporate clients often require certification and references and will want to meet you in person to make certain you're the right fit for their organizations. *Make sure that you are preparing yourself for the opportunities you want.*

Unlike established professions that have licenses that are regulated by the government, you don't have to be a licensed coach: coaching is unregulated. In the following sections, I want to help you understand how this impacts the field of coaching by exploring the differences among credentials, such as the individual certification and program accreditation.

Diagram 6: Certification and Accreditation

CERTIFICATION   ACCREDITATION

*A **certification** is for an individual coach whereas **accreditation** is for a coach training program.*
(Note: In Europe, the term "accreditation" is used interchangeably to describe both.)

CREDENTIAL

Just like you would know that you're getting a specific level of quality when you go to the doctor's office, credentials exist to ensure that coaches have a certain competency level of proficiency (based on the requirements of the organization awarding the designation) and protection for consumers. In most professions, there is usually a central association that certifies its members. In coaching there are both associations and independent businesses that credential individuals, and each one has a different viewpoint on the competencies and qualifications needed for coaching.

There are several associations and organizations that offer individual credentials and are well known in the field. The International Coach Federation (ICF), the International Association of Coaching (IAC), the Worldwide Association of Business Coaches (WABC), and the Center for Credentialing and Education (CCE) all offer designations to individuals and programs. In Europe, the well-known organizations are the European Mentoring and Coaching Council (EMCC) and the Association for Coaching (AC).

These organizations have requirements for coaching proficiencies (what makes a good coach), codes of ethics, and certification requirements. There are benefits to individual membership such as standards to guide your work, resources, networking, continuing education programs, and other support for coaches (e.g., discounted insurance plans). They differ in their philosophies, their belief of what makes a qualified coach, and the type of training required. There are also different processes to apply and reapply for the credential.

I've included additional information on these organizations in the following sections as well as in Part V, which you'll want to review, as you look into what credentialing organization best fits your needs and your belief system.

CERTIFICATION

Many coach training programs offer varying levels of training as well as certification options, so the program you graduate from may certify you. Each of the individual coach training programs sets its own certification standards, which are tied to the curriculum and requirements of the individual program. For example, if you graduate from Presence-Based Leadership Development's Coaching Training, you will become a Certified Presence-Based Coach. If you graduate from Martha Beck's Life Coach Training, you will become a Certified Martha Beck Life Coach. The list goes on.

While these certifications may stand on their own, many graduates choose to also apply for an individual credential, or designation, through one of the recognized coaching associations.

CERTIFICATE OF COMPLETION

A certificate of completion indicates you've completed the specific requirements of a program. UT Dallas offers a Graduate Certificate in Executive and Professional Coaching. The Neuro-Leadership Group offers a Brain-Based Coaching Certificate. Any program can offer a certificate of completion whether it's one day or one hundred days long. Because the quality varies widely, a certificate program may be just as in-depth as a certification program. Or certificate programs could be severely lacking in substance.

If you wanted, you could print up a certificate of completion for reading this book. It's easy to award a certificate, and it's important to understand what it stands for.

While a certificate of completion may stand on its own as evidence of specific training, many graduates choose to also apply for an individual credential, or designation, through one of the recognized coaching associations.

> *Certification is one way of showing that you have a certain level of skill, knowledge, and expertise. It doesn't prove that you're a great coach, but it does demonstrate that you have a grounding in the discipline. That's very important in a field where anyone can legally hang out a shingle. There's a lot that goes into being a great coach, and investing the time and dedication required for the right training and practice is essential."*

—Janet Crawford, founder, Cascadance

ACCREDITATION OF TRAINING PROGRAMS

People who search for accredited programs may associate accreditation with credibility; however, not all accreditation systems are created equal! If the program you're looking into is accredited, make sure it is accredited by a reputable organization that passes your smell test. Also, check with other coaches whom you talk with about the value of being affiliated with an accrediting organization.

If a program is accredited by an association, you may want to ask yourself the following questions:

- Who is the accrediting association and what is its philosophy on coaching?
- How long has the association been in existence?
- Who is running the association and accrediting programs?
- What are the standards that guide accreditation? How transparent are those standards?
- How often are the standards updated to reflect the changing marketplace?

Being accredited often reflects the program's commitment to abide by specific industry standards. Becoming accredited can be time-consuming and costs money, so not all programs decide to invest in the process. Meanwhile, some programs decide not to become accredited because they don't agree with the approach or philosophy of abiding by someone else's coaching standards. It's helpful to understand whether a coach training program is not accredited because of a differing opinion or lack of appetite to put in the time and effort.

At the time of this writing, coaching associations and organizations have different approaches toward accreditation. The International Coach Federation (ICF) accredits programs based on their own competencies. The International Association of Coaching (IAC) offers licenses to programs that use IAC Coaching Masteries. The Worldwide Association of Business Coaches (WABC) accredits programs based on its standards of business coaching. The Center for Credentialing and Education (CCE) does not accredit programs but approves trainings that are eligible to be counted toward the Board Certified Coach (BCC) designation.

Coaches in the field have compared these coaching associations/organizations to subgroups or commissions within specific organizations such as the American Psychological Association (APA) or the American Society for Training & Development (ASTD).

It's also worth mentioning two additional organizations that do not accredit training programs but rather focus more on supporting and advocating for training programs. The Graduate School Alliance for Executive Coaching (GSAEC) is specifically for graduate-level certification and degree programs. The Association of Coach Training Organizations (ACTO) is a consortium of (mostly ICF) accredited programs that work together to support collaboration across coach training programs.

Note: *There are differing opinions and questions being asked about the future of coaching accreditation. What defines an association? Can an association credential both individuals and accredit organizations? Who is accrediting the accreditors? I encourage you to visit Peer Resources, an online peer network of information, to explore these topics further. You can also look into the other magazines and websites listed in the Resources section to learn more.*

AFFILIATIONS

Depending on your ambitions, consider what affiliations and/or partnerships each program has. Some programs are connected to universities or research institutes, while others operate independently. This may impact the options and opportunities you have to connect with resources and people.

For example, Columbia's Coaching Certification Program (CCCP) is affiliated with the Executive Education division of Columbia Business School as well as the Center for Educational Outreach and Innovation at Columbia's Teachers College.

Some of these programs provide additional benefits such as access to a university's graduate community or the option to apply your coaching training to the requirements for a higher education degree. Others associate with an institute that is a center for research and advanced learning such as Integral Coaching Canada (with the Integral Institute) and Coaches Training Institute, CTI (with the Institute of Coaching at McLean Hospital, a Harvard Medical School Affiliate).

DIFFERENT APPROACHES TO COACHING

2. DIFFERENT APPROACHES TO COACHING

The program's approach or philosophy will define the program's general offering or specialization, as well as the curriculum. It will also directly link to the coaching models and supporting tools and templates it provides.

PHILOSOPHY

A program's philosophy—the disciplines and theories that influence the program—is the primary reason most coaches select one program over another. This will be the lens through which coaching skills are taught. It could also relate to whether the program is multidisciplinary and what fields it draws on.

Some programs focus on a general approach (think liberal arts), and other programs are more specialized. As you explore your interests, you may choose to focus on a general coaching approach or you may choose a specific lens (through mind, body, spirit, team coaching, etc.).

I've listed several of these specialized lenses below:

- **Mind:** focus on how our brains are wired and the connection between thoughts and behavior; may also include mindfulness

- **Body:** focus on "somatics," how you can coach using the body, and how it influences and reinforces behaviors; may also include "presence" and "embodiment"

- **Spirit:** focus on the higher meaning or purpose of our existence (may or may not be religious in nature)

- **Organizational/Team Coaching:** focus on systems thinking and team dynamics; coaching within groups/teams and/or organizations

Philosophy also applies to the founders and key coaching leaders who have shaped the coach training program. Who are the founders? What are their backgrounds, and what do they bring to the program? How are they involved in the program and how do they help the program evolve?

Some programs teach both the theory and the application of coaching. Others focus on application but will not delve into theory. Often academic-based or evidence-based programs (which draw on research and theory) focus on both theory and application.

If a program is based in an academic setting, consider where the coach training program is housed (e.g., the psychology department or the business school).

Note: *Which program philosophy is ideal for you is very much connected to how you view the world. Certain approaches and theories will resonate with you, and others won't. If you can, locate a video of the program on YouTube or the program website and watch it to get a sense of how you feel about what is being said. Check out the bios of the founders and read their articles and/or books to get a sense of their approaches and philosophies on life. Often, the primary book or article written by the program's founder will be a prerequisite for the program itself. I've included each program's marquis book/article in the "Coaching Resources" section.*

Tanisha Drummer Parrish, a graduate of the Coaches Training Institute (CTI), wanted a holistic approach to coaching. She selected CTI because of its philosophy and the reputation of its book "Co-Active Coaching." The program also fit into her schedule, as she balanced a full-time corporate job. She is grateful for how the training is structured to be experiential rather than academic—and how it facilitated her personal transformation related to relationships, happiness, and life purpose.

A Word about Founders: Many programs' founders are still thriving, researching, and adding their experience to the broader coaching field. Revised handbooks and new editions of published books are rewritten to account for the changing landscape of coaching and the global marketplace. Many founders are responsible for informing the strategic direction of programs, updating program content, and serving as faculty/instructors. Moreover, some are involved with associations and broader conversations around the future of coaching.

Note: *It is valuable to know who developed the training program's content and who continues to update it on a regular basis. The field of coaching is constantly evolving, and some programs are better at adapting the latest research and needs from the marketplace. You might be able to meet key leaders and coaching pioneers in person at trainings, conferences, or summits.*

COACHING MODELS AND METHODOLOGIES

Each program offers slightly different models, which provide the high-level strategy for coaching, and methodology, which details the steps in a coaching session. How do you contract and set up the coaching engagement (the agreement that covers the number of sessions and frequency of meetings with your client)? What is discussed in coaching sessions, and what are the beginning, middle, and end steps?

Each program has a perspective on how the coach works with clients, whether it's creating analogies to illuminate the client's concern or helping the client overcome self-imposed obstacles to success. Some programs provide you with the methodology to frame your coaching approach but are not necessarily prescriptive in identifying what tools and exercises will support your coaching. Other programs have a more prescriptive approach to how you work with clients.

In some cases, programs clearly lay out what coaching methodology you will use and how it is applicable. With other programs, you have to go through the program and the process to understand what steps are best taken in a coaching engagement.

> *Paraphrasing Lois Jewel Barber, the Co-creator and Executive Director of EarthAction, going through a program is like origami—it all makes sense after you go through it and really see how the twists and turns happened and what you have accomplished."*

—Rita Brown, Integral Master Coach
(Integral Coaching Canada Inc.)

Note: *Depending on the program, you may or may not have to pay a licensing fee to use the program materials afterward. Know what your intention is and learn what the program includes. Tactically speaking, if you are going to run a workshop using the content you receive through the program, will you be able to cite the original reference, and/or will you need to pay to use that material? On top of that, will the content apply to the audience you're targeting? Life coaching content, for example, might not translate for the business community.*

Mary Elizabeth Murphy, owner of S.T.A.R. Resources, is a graduate of CRR Global and the Coaches Training Institute (CTI). During a twenty-year career, she has transitioned from a trainer to a facilitator to a consultant to what she describes as a coach-consultant. She chose to do coach training through CRR Global because of its focus on systems and team coaching as well as the in-person, interactive setting. Mary is grateful for what she learned at CRR Global about relationships and accessing the system as a whole. She is currently a registered licensee of CRR Global's Relationship Systems Intelligence RSI@Work Process that she uses with clients.

CURRICULUM

Each coach training program has its own curriculum based on its philosophy and approach to coaching. For example, most programs will cover the ethics and competencies for coaches as well as the coaching flow and subsequent models, methodologies, and tools/exercises that it supports. The level of group and individual activities will vary, as well as the self-development focus. The program may also require a final assignment or capstone project.

Depending on how academic or evidence-based the program is, the curriculum may cover theories that inform coaching. Programs with a specific lens or focus may go into detail about related theories or ideas that are most relevant. For example, George Mason University's Advanced Coach Training Program in Leadership and Well-Being focuses on developing well-being coaches. Its six modules focus on positive psychology, mindfulness, mindful presence, mindful transitions, polarity thinking, and conflict as opportunity. Other programs that bring in a mind, body, spirit, or organizational lens will also provide a deeper level of understanding about these topics.

Life coach programs often have a slightly different approach and tend to address a set of topic areas (e.g., relationships/family, work, passion), so individuals will feel comfortable coaching around these issues. They accomplish this by bringing in resources and sometimes even doing field trips to help potential coaches get more comfortable coaching around specific topics.

Note: *Most programs clearly share their curriculum on their websites, and it's helpful to further research so that you know exactly what is included in a given coach training program.*

Rita Brown, *a graduate of Integral Coaching Canada's Coaching Certification Program, selected Integral Coaching Canada's program because it is grounded in an integral approach and adult development theory. The program is highly rigorous and encourages coaches to become fully embodied—the curriculum spans mind, body, heart, and spirit. Since completing the program, Rita serves as a mentor and has been grateful for the strong community in the San Francisco area, the yearly events, and the ongoing exchanges online.*

A Word about Capstone Projects: Some programs (such as the Columbia Coaching Certification Program and CRR Global's ORSC Coaching Certification Program) require a personal project involving research on a coaching-related topic that interests you. This is usually in addition to the requirements of oral and written exams. Certain programs provide access to the different papers on their websites.

ACCESS TO COACHING COLLEAGUES

3. ACCESS TO COACHING COLLEAGUES

You'll have access to participants in your actual program, the instructors/faculty who will support you in your learning, and the extended alumni community. Below I highlight examples from coach training programs to help you think about connections with coaching colleagues and the implications for your coaching practice.

INSTRUCTORS/FACULTY

Your instructors or faculty will set the tone for the program. This ties into what type of learning environment best supports your needs, as instructors can make or break the experience. Many programs require their instructors to have a minimum number of years of training and a full- or part-time coaching practice, as well as certification from a recognized coaching program or association.

It's helpful to know whether you will have the same faculty throughout the program or if they will rotate. There are benefits and drawbacks to both, but I tend to find that the more coaches you are exposed to, the clearer your decision will be about whether to emulate them—or run away from them. Some programs have two faculty members who facilitate jointly and often will have upwards of seven or eight instructors to expose participants to different coaching styles.

Some programs will place additional people in the room or on the phone to support your learning experience. This may be in the form of mentors and assistants who will also be a part of your learning experience.

Note: *You can review faculty profiles before you apply to the program. It's tough to gauge whether the instructors have the know-how to create a great learning experience. As a starter, you can make sure that they have experience you value and relevant training. Make note of whether the faculty/instructors are academics/PhDs, practitioners, or otherwise. Also, as you start to connect with programs and alumni who have graduated from coach training programs, ask them about their firsthand experience with the instructors.*

PEER GROUP

Each coach training program tends to have a diverse mix of individuals with different goals, and individual motivations for attending vary quite a bit. Some want personal development and growth and have no intention of becoming coaches. Some people want to become professional coaches and create thriving practices. Others want to use coaching as a leadership tool for change initiatives or take coaching skills back to their organizations.

On the whole, life coaching programs have traditionally attracted more women, while business/executive coaching programs have attracted a more balanced mix of genders. This may be a reflection of the learning culture and/or the tendency for women to be attracted to more empathetic fields (a topic for a whole different book!).

The international diversity of program attendees is growing, while at the same time, programs are expanding overseas in partnership with other organizations or affiliates. The broader alumni network may include individuals around the globe and may shift based on where the coach training program expands.

Some programs make it a point to have people with different experiences in the course in order to add a variety of perspectives; other programs assign groups based on who has signed up. Each coach training program approaches this process differently. This is reflected in the application process, which varies from asking participants to fill out a form and submit a payment to scheduling a phone conversation to filling out a comprehensive application.

Consider: do you want to be part of a cohort model that is going through the coach training program together? Or are you okay with new people entering and taking the courses alongside you (if the course is structured in a set of modules)? This is another factor for consideration.

Note: *If you are doing business locally, you may want to think about what connections you'll obtain through the coach training program. Consider where you'll be living and/or working and whether the coaches in your network will be able to support you in the way you want.*

ALUMNI COMMUNITY

Three aspects of the alumni community can greatly impact your future success as a coach: resources, referrals, and partnerships.

The networks and coaches you know will impact your ability to access resources such as coaching discussion boards and tools, templates, and practices to support your coaching engagements. Secondly, many alumni groups have active networks and communities that share coaching opportunities and engagements. This impacts the clients who are referred to you as coaches who are networked with each other will refer clients to each other. Lastly, coaches looking to partner with other coaches often start within the community they know the best. Therefore, if you're looking for a thought partner or another coach to collaborate with, you will be able to access your peer group and potentially reach out to the alumni community as an easy starting point.

You can find resources, referral groups, and partnerships in a number of ways. The top coaching programs provide quality alumni services, such as local and national networking groups (sometimes small groups will form organically) as well as communities of practice, LISTSERVes, and websites. These websites will list credentialed coaches from their programs and up-to-date information on research and publications, resources, and local and national events.

Note: *Some coach training programs have more active alumni programs and services than others, which is often advertised on the program's website. When you speak with coaches who have completed a program, make sure to understand what's available to alumni and whether or not the community website or e-mail list is active. This offering can make or break the support you will have if and when you start a coaching business.*

Melissa Scott, a graduate of iPEC, selected the coach certification program because she connected with the core energy coaching philosophy, liked the mixture of classroom and virtual time to manage her personal/work demands and also the timeline of the program. Melissa walked away with her requirements for ICF certification (she is now an Associated Certified Coach), the skills to start coaching, and an "extended family of coaches with all types of niches." She noted, "It really impacted the way I see the world and people, providing me with what I have found to be essential for successfully managing my personal life/thinking and coaching others."

A CONTINUOUS LEARNING ENVIRONMENT

4. A CONTINUOUS LEARNING ENVIRONMENT

Does the program learning environment work for you? In this section I expand on learning approaches, coaching practice, and other learning opportunities.

LEARNING APPROACH

The learning approach is often linked to how the program is delivered, which I discuss in the Program Logistics section. Some programs are set up specifically with adult learners in mind, and others are simply set up to facilitate learning.

On the whole, most programs are structured to enable you to have a shared learning experience. This creates a learning environment where individuals can share their coaching challenges and questions in a more intimate setting. This might mean that, within your program's group or cohort, you are part of a smaller subgroup, such as a pod or learning circle. This is usually the same across virtual and in-person programs.

Many programs also ask that you find a buddy or a learning partner to work with during the program. You may or may not coach this person, depending on how the coaching practice is orchestrated.

Note: *Consider the size of the program. Many programs deliberately keep their cohorts small; some programs have eight people, while others keep it to less than twenty-five. If this is important to you, look into the size of a program's learning group and how it will be structured to support your learning needs.*

COACHING PRACTICE

The key focus in coach training programs is to learn how to coach and there is usually ample time to apply what you are learning and practice coaching. Most programs require you to complete coaching hours and/or take on a specific number of coaching clients as part of the curriculum. The number of clients you're required to coach, the hours you need to put in, and the documentation of case studies differs across programs.

Lack of confidence can be a huge barrier for new coaches to break through. Practicing your coaching and getting feedback helps to build your confidence. It provides the assurance you are meeting the competencies needed for coaching. Even if you complete a coach training program, confidence as a coach takes time to develop (sounds like a coachable issue!).

Note: *Some programs have you practice peer coaching with individuals in the program. Others ask you to take on paid or pro bono clients outside of your program.*

Before becoming a coach, Denise Bray, now a graduate of New Ventures West, had met James Flaherty (the founder of New Ventures West) and was familiar with his work. She had also worked with a coach in her HR career. As she looked into coaching programs, she was interested in the somatic (body), spiritual, and integral components of New Ventures West in San Francisco, where she lives. She recalls the first weekend this way: "Each person gets coached live in front of the class. It's extremely powerful and exposes you to the New Ventures West style of coaching." During the program, she was invited to explore a practice of painting with watercolors as a way to tap into her creativity. Denise is grateful for the teachers and the style of the program, as well as the learning community.

ADVANCED COACHING PRACTICE

Many programs offer their alumni some type of continuing education focused on learning higher-level coaching techniques (advanced coaching). This may be in the form of workshops or an advanced coach training program for experienced coaches. Coaching supervision and mentor coaching, which train coaches to become supervisors and mentors, are also being developed as advanced trainings by programs.

Note: *Coaching supervision, which is more commonly practiced in Europe, is still emerging in the United States. It is likely an area that both programs and associations will pay more attention to in the future in support of developing quality coaches.*

OTHER LEARNING OPPORTUNITIES

Many programs offer an annual summit or conference for alumni that includes keynotes, breakout sessions, and workshops on coaching-related topics. Some coach training programs offer alumni retreats and/or publicize relevant trainings sponsored by the programs.

There may be opportunities to mentor in the classroom, serve as an advisor, and even take facilitator/faculty training after you complete a coach training program.

Note: *It's helpful to consider what type of coaching trajectory you anticipate. If you start at one program (and you like it), you may want to continue taking advanced courses to further your knowledge of the program's models and approach to coaching. There is always the opportunity to take different courses through other programs.*

FOCUS ON DEVELOPING YOURSELF

5. FOCUS ON DEVELOPING YOURSELF

A coach training program provides tools and exercises that will support you as "self as coach" to create awareness around your own personal development. These are the same tools and exercises that you may choose to use with your clients.

Within a coach training program, the ability for you to work on yourself is directly tied to your personal investment in yourself. It is also tied to the amount of coaching and mentoring support you will receive from the faculty and your peers.

The process of taking the time and space to self-reflect during your program can be quite powerful on its own. When you add in a controlled environment that prioritizes self-reflection, the experience of being coached, and the ability to practice coaching exercises on yourself, the result can be transformative.

SELF-TRANSFORMATION

The degree of self-transformation you experience can be attributed to the way the program is set up. Certain programs are specifically designed for coaches to do the work on themselves. This might include a personal development or learning plan that you create at the beginning of the program. It might also include time and space for personal reflection, ongoing practices, exercises, journaling, and other activities to self-reflect and grow.

The degree of self-transformation is highly attributable to you. The amount of effort and time you invest in working on yourself directly impacts your ability to be a good coach. Think about a coach or mentor that you have had. What makes him or her good? What would you hope that your coach or mentor does for his or her own personal development?

Note: *To be a great coach, you need to do the work yourself. It is critical for coaches to work on themselves so that they can create a space for others to work on themselves. While you can certainly work on this on your own, it's helpful to choose a program that reflects this self-growth/transformational component.*

RECEIVE COACHING

Most programs will offer you the opportunity to receive coaching, whether by a mentor coach or a peer coach. A mentor coach (a term often used by programs accredited by the International Coach Federation) is someone who provides you with feedback on your coaching by listening to recordings of your coaching sessions. This person may also provide you with actual coaching as well.

Some people don't like the term "mentor coach" because it blurs the distinctions between mentoring and coaching, two different concepts. Mentoring is about providing guidance and expertise based on experience, while coaching is about helping people find their own answers by asking the right questions. Mentor coaches in some programs do both—they might coach and mentor you.

If you receive coaching as part of the program, you will typically get coached on your coaching ability and on any personal topics you're working on. If you are submitting recordings of your coaching sessions for review, your mentor coach will provide feedback on your coaching style and approach (usually in accordance with the competencies outlined by the program itself or the accrediting organization).

I don't want to totally confuse you with terminology, but I do want to highlight that some programs, like Georgetown's Leadership Coaching Certificate Program, match you up with a mentor from the broader alumni group in addition to the person coaching you. This mentor might be someone with similar experience who is interested in sharing his or her coaching knowledge and best practices with you as a new coach.

Note: *A few programs let you choose your own coach in order to model what it's like to be in your client's shoes, while others assign you a coach. Many programs have you do peer coaching, in which someone from your program practices coaching on you (and vice versa). There are benefits and drawbacks to peer coaching—you may benefit from these coaching interactions in learning what you do and don't want to do as a coach. You may, however, be lacking the model coaching that you could receive from an experienced coach. You will want to clarify who the coach is and what his or her role will be. You will also want to clarify how many hours of coaching you will receive and if the coaching is included in the price of the program or you have to pay out of pocket.*

SUPPORT TO LAUNCH A COACHING BUSINESS

6. SUPPORT TO LAUNCH A COACHING BUSINESS

If you're considering using a coach training program as a launching pad for a business, you may or may not need to look for outside help. There is a burgeoning business for coaches who help other coaches launch their own businesses—and there's good reason.

The level of support that programs offer for getting your business up and running varies widely. Some programs will spend an hour on the topic, and others will support you with full back-office support, client introduction packets, managing client payments, and more.

Programs that provide support to help you launch a coaching practice may focus on logistics (as compared to strategy and execution) such as forming a business entity, legally protecting yourself, and accepting methods of payments online.

Many coaches network with marketers and brand strategists to develop their businesses. To respond to market needs, programs are starting to offer business-related training as an add-on through their alumni and/or continuing education programs.

Note: *Depending on the coaching philosophy, certain programs differentiate between being a good coach and a good businessperson, which don't always go* *together. If you want help with launching your own business as part of the program, consider a life coaching program or one that provides more support in this area. Otherwise, prepare to invest in additional training and/or coaching to start your practice.*

PROGRAM LOGISTICS

In addition to the benefits of coach training programs, it's important to think through program logistics related to timing and when course sessions take place. Other considerations include the location of the training and how it is delivered.

Virtual or In Person

There are quality programs that are designed for virtual environments, in-person learning, or a combination of the two. Deciding on the best option for you will be a question of your learning preference and schedule/availability. Many programs have invested in virtual classroom environments, and as you probably know, twenty-first-century learning environments can make it feel as though you're actually meeting in person. Many coaches who have experienced online training are amazed by the deep levels of listening in conversations held over the phone and in virtual learning environments.

At the same time, there is something to be said for in-person learning sessions fostering personal relationships on a different level than online relationships. Be sure to understand when you will be meeting in person and when you will meet online.

Note: *If the program meets in person, you can gauge the program's style by how the classroom is set up and where it is located. Your program might sit in a circle to facilitate a more intimate community, or it might be conducted in classrooms with square desks if you've decided to attend an academic lecture-style program. If you decide to enroll in a program that takes place in a retreatlike environment or out in nature, your setup might be a bit more adventurous.*

Location of Training

If you're considering a program with in-person classes, look into where the program is offered. The boutique or smaller training programs are often offered where the staff and organization are headquartered. The larger programs offer their trainings in major cities, and often with partners or affiliates around the globe. It is helpful to consider how the location of your training impacts the type of people who are in the training with you, specifically around how these individuals can help support you locally, nationally, and globally depending on where you live and work.

Note: *If your first language is not English and you are considering programs in other languages, keep in mind who your target population is. If you are going to be coaching Spanish speakers, then it might be advantageous to learn coaching in Spanish.*

Program Structure and Timing

Programs tend to offer entry into their training multiple times a year. Trainings may be held on predetermined days of the month (such as the weekend or weekdays) or at regular weekly meetings (e.g., on Mondays or Wednesdays). Usually there is some consistency around cadence (weekly or monthly), day(s), and timing. There are also programs that conduct their training sequentially at various points in the year. In this scenario, you can enroll in each of the training courses/modules depending on when they are offered.

In terms of program duration, some coach training programs are weekend certificates, and others last six to twelve months. You're not going to become a great coach in a weekend. You might pick up some skills and techniques you can apply to your everyday practice, but you're not going to master the art of coaching. It takes time to integrate your learning experience and incorporate a new way of thinking and doing into your everyday actions.

Note: *It's worth looking into the timing of the program early in this process—both when you can apply during the year and what days and times are available. If the programs are offered as sequential trainings, you may be able to take an accelerated version of the training.*

Anabel Suárez, an executive and organizational coach, is a graduate of the Columbia Coaching Certification Program. She decided to attend a coach training program that would help her with techniques to use with her existing coaching clients. Anabel selected Columbia because of its structure *and format. Flying from her home in the Canary Islands, Spain, to New York was a long distance, and she liked that the program kicked off with an intensive two weeks in person followed by virtual sessions. Other reasons Anabel selected the program were its reputation, prestige, and faculty. She enjoyed the topics she studied at Columbia and the experience of presenting a capstone research project.*

INVESTING IN YOUR COACH TRAINING

You will need to invest time, effort, and money in your training, and the importance of these commitments will vary by program. I've expanded on these considerations below.

Time and Effort Required

It's helpful to understand what the basic requirements are for the program so that you know what to expect in terms of time commitment. This may or may not reflect the true number of hours needed to complete the program work, so you will want to compare these numbers with what past program participants share with you about their experience. Consider using the program requirements as a minimum. The more effort you are able to put into the program, the more you'll get out of it.

What many people overlook is the amount of time coach training programs take, especially considering the number of hours you will be coaching. Think about how you are going to manage a coach training program with the everyday demands of your life. Some people continue to work full-time, while others move to part-time schedules or take personal leaves/sabbaticals to do the work.

Note: *Programs tend to have policies on missing a training course or online module. Some programs video record live classes or telecourses, which are then made available afterward to enrolled individuals.*

Understand the Costs

The price tag is not the best way to select a program, as the cost usually reflects the duration of the program and the value associated with it. Programs that are similar in length (and quality) often have similar price tags, which won't help you to differentiate between them. What is helpful to consider is what is included in the price of a program and what is excluded. Expenses that may not be included are the cost of a coach, course materials, and travel expenses. The additional costs of staying in a hotel or a rented apartment add up, so clarify the actual dollar amount you will be spending.

As I mentioned earlier, coach training programs will ask that you take on a specific number of clients or complete a specific number of coaching hours. Find out whether these sessions can be paid hours, as there is a possibility that you can earn back your coaching tuition as you practice your coaching.

Note: *Some programs offer a full refund for the course you've taken if it is not working for you. Other programs offer you the option to take the program again after you've completed it—at no additional charge—if you want to freshen up your coaching skills. There are often a variety of payment options available through the program, so don't hesitate to ask for what you need.*

Academic Credit and Continuing Education

If you work for an organization that has tuition reimbursement, you may want to consider what type of academic credits are available to you. For example, Coaches Training Institute (CTI) has an affiliation with the American Council on Education (ACE), which recommends university-level credits for CTI's courses that students can receive as college credits.

Also, some programs support continuing education credits. For example, New Ventures West is associated with the California Board of Behavioral Sciences (BBS), which supports counseling professionals in California as they maintain their licenses.

Note: *If you work for an organization, find out if your employer sends individuals to specific coach training programs. Your employer may also financially support selected individuals to receive coach training.*

Based on what you have read about logistics, take the time to think about what works best for you. This is a good time to take stock of how much time and effort you have to invest in a program. Also, it's helpful to think about whether a virtual or in-person program is feasible for you and how it aligns to your learning style. Using the questions below as a guide, write down your thoughts on logistics.

Location:

Based on schedule, cost, and personal preference, how important is it that you do a coach training program in person or that you don't have to travel?

_____
_____
_____

If you do the program in person, do you want to do it locally?

_____
_____
_____

Cost:

How much money are you able to invest in a training program, keeping in mind that you might be able to pay for part of the program with paying clients?

___

If you work within an organization, is there a possibility of training reimbursement in any form?

___

Available Time/Schedule:

Realistically, how much time do you have to devote to a coach training program?

___

What actions, if any, do you need to take to support your desire to do a coach training program?

___

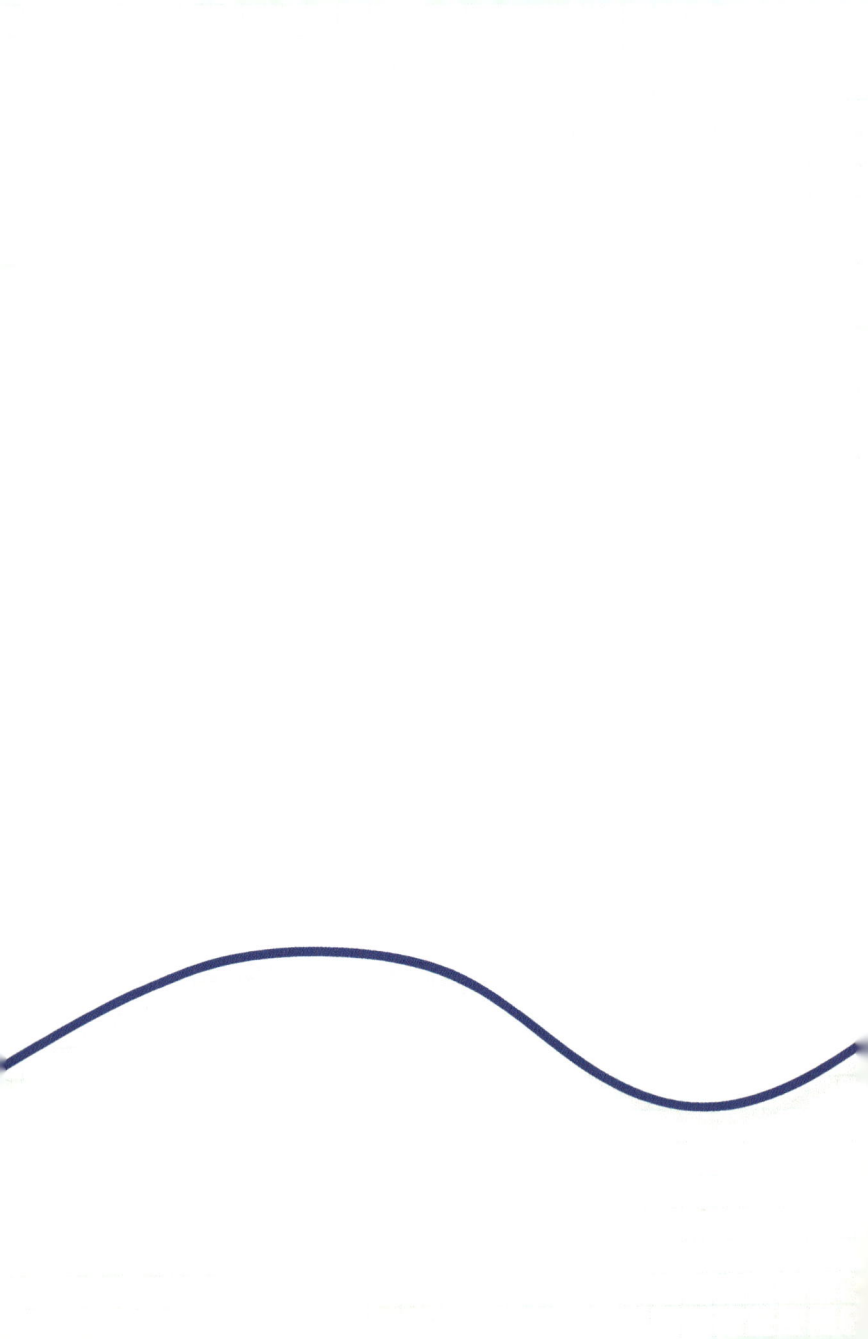

PART IV
FIND THE COACH TRAINING PROGRAM THAT BEST FITS YOUR NEEDS

PART IV

In this section I help you to think about which program best fits your needs. I discuss ways that you can conduct research, including interviewing coaches and staff, take an introductory course, and do your best to recognize when the program fit feels right.

At the end of this section is a detailed worksheet that summarizes Part III ("What You Need to Know about Coaching") into an easy guide with questions you can reference as you talk to training programs and their graduate coaches.

It is important to select a program that matches the kind of coaching you're interested in and the type of clients you want to work with. The focus of the program should ideally relate to the type of clients you want to coach. For instance, if you are going into a program known for its focus on leadership, many of the case examples will relate to this context. Also, the clients you coach during the program will need to be in leadership roles. If you're interested in holistic/life coaching, then you might thrive in a program that uses more whole-person examples (even though it may bring in leadership or organizational references).

A Yiddish expression comes to mind: "There's a seat for every tuchus, and a tuchus for every seat." In other words, whatever your needs and interests, there is a program out there that is right for you. And if there isn't, you can start to create your own developmental path to support you in your coaching journey.

DO YOUR RESEARCH

One easy way to begin is to take stock of the successful coaches you have observed and look at what credentials and training they have done. Talk to your network of contacts, and if you have a coach, ask him or her for a recommendation on training programs. Visit the coaching association websites in Part V to find up-to-date lists of programs.

One more thing: Do your research, but don't let it cripple you. You will want to balance what you learn from your research with your intuition. Sometimes your intuition or gut feeling is right. As you research and learn about the options, stay focused on your priorities and the best choice for you.

- Who in your network do you feel is knowledgeable about options for coach training programs?
- Which leaders or coaches have you seen that you respect and want to learn from? What credentials and training do they have?
- What models and methodologies have you used or do you want to use as a coach?

INTERVIEW COACHES AND PROGRAM STAFF

Nearly every program offers live or recorded informational calls with representatives of the program and/or graduates of the program. These informational calls can help you narrow down which program is the best fit for you.

Note: *Pay attention to the personalities of the individuals representing a given program. Many of the administrative staff will have completed the program and know firsthand what the experience is like. Also, their language and way of interacting with you will provide perspective about what the program will be like and how you might sound to others one day.*

Sheppard Lake, *a graduate of the Martha Beck Life Coach Training Program, knew within five minutes of an introductory call that Martha Beck's program was the right fit. The idea of stepping out of traditional, formulaic models and having the flexibility to make the tools her own resonated with Sheppard. She is grateful for the self-awareness and personal discovery and the close ties she formed through the virtual training. Since graduating, Sheppard has continued to coach individuals and groups. In addition, she incorporates these tools in her work with organizations.*

SAMPLE THE PROGRAM

Participating in a workshop is a great way to "try on" the program before you commit. It also exposes you to the different approaches, exercises, styles, and techniques the program offers. Many programs want to try out their applicants as much as the applicants want to try out the programs. These programs might offer a three- or four-day experiential workshop to highlight the program's preferred tools and ways of thinking, and sometimes serve as a prerequisite or entry point to the broader certification program.

Sometimes these introductory courses are available in two flavors: one for entry-level coaches and one for more experienced coaches. There may also be a complimentary course or workshop that provides an introduction to coaching like the Hudson Institute of Coaching's LifeLaunch and Coaching Seminar.

__Laura Westman__, a graduate of Accomplishment Coaching's Coaches' Training Program, selected the program after attending an observation of the training, a unique opportunity to experience the program firsthand. The content and experience of the observation resonated with Laura and empowered her to take action in her own life. She is grateful for how the training created a space for active exploration, support in the form of weekly coaching, and back-office *support for affiliates of the program. Since completing the program, Laura has achieved her desired outcome of becoming a full-time coach, and she also serves as a mentor coach for Accomplishment Coaching's programs in Kuala Lumpur, Malaysia, and New York.*

Note: *Participating in coaching workshops and trainings exposes you to different coaching models and approaches. This is not only a great way to sample programs, but also a way to gain targeted content knowledge to build your skill set and network.*

KNOW WHEN IT FEELS RIGHT

As you make your decision, think about your own worldview and how a given program reflects your values and meets your coaching needs. If you prefer a more action-oriented or outcomes-driven approach and you're working with executives who like that perspective, then a program focusing on driving solutions may appeal to you. If you're empathetic and derive knowledge from your body wisdom or intuition and that is part of the value you offer to your client, then a program focusing on this softer or more intuitive approach may be a good fit.

Here are some ideas to consider as you gauge what program feels right:

- Do you relate to the program's philosophy or approach to coaching?

- Does the language the program uses intrigue and/or excite you?
- How well do you connect with the coaches and program administrators that you've spoken with? Are these people you can see as part of your network in the future?
- Are there any parts of the program that make you feel skeptical or that don't seem practical to you?

Take the time you need to do your research, interview coaches and program staff, and sample the programs, when possible. You might come back to these questions from time to time as you actively explore your options.

Christine Calandrella, *a graduate of NeuroLeadership's Certificate in Brain-Based Coaching program has worked in human resources for over fifteen years. As she looked into coaching programs, someone recommended that she read* Your Brain at Work *by David Rock. After reading the book, she wanted to learn more and decided to take the introductory six-week telecourse shortly after. "It totally revolutionized my approach to coaching. I learned how to leverage what we know about the brain to help people achieve new insights." She is grateful for the personal transformation and coaching approach she learned in the process.*

WORKSHEET:
GUIDED QUESTIONS FOR SELECTING A COACH TRAINING PROGRAM

The table below includes a summarized list of the topics discussed in the book, presented in order of importance. Many coach training programs provide the answers to these questions on their websites. You can use this table to help you think through which questions you want to have answered.

Before you read through the questions, take the time to write down your top priorities in a coaching program. Considering your answers to the questions on location, cost, and time in Part III, write down your response to the questions below.

What are your top three to five priorities?

_____
_____
_____

What is a must-have or nonnegotiable for you in a coach training program?

___

___

___

How will you know when the program feels right for you?

___

___

___

GUIDED QUESTIONS FOR SELECTING A COACH TRAINING PROGRAM

Factors	Questions to Ask Yourself	Questions You May Want to Ask Programs
DIFFERENT APPROACHES TO COACHING		
Philosophy	What theories and disciplines am I interested in learning about?	How does the program define its coaching approach?
	Do I want to approach coaching more generally or focus on a specific area of expertise?	Is the program based on the philosophy of a specific thought leader or approach?
	How important is it that a program's founder be a leading expert or voice in the coaching field?	Is the program multidisciplinary? What is the mix of theory and application?

Coaching Models and Methodology	What types of models/methodologies do I need to support me in my coaching?	Does the program have a coaching model? Who created it? Does the program have a coaching methodology? Who created it?
Curriculum	What do I want to learn?	What is the curriculum?
ACCESS TO COACHING COLLEAGUES		
Instructors/ Faculty	What diversity of experience and background is important to me? Do I identify with the instructors and their experience (based on their CVs or bios)?	What are the requirements for instructors? What training and/or credentials are required? Years of experience? Coaching practice? Are the faculty members recognized thought leaders who have published material? Do the faculty stay the same throughout the course, or do they rotate?
Peer Group	What type of community do I want to belong to? Is it important for me to grow my network locally, nationally, or internationally?	What type of people does the program attract? What are their backgrounds and interests in coaching? How rigorous is the program's application process?

Alumni Community	What do I want to access from the alumni community?	What do graduates typically do after the coaching program? What alumni opportunities does the program offer?
A CONTINUOUS LEARNING ENVIRONMENT		
Learning	What type of learning environment is important to me? What type of advanced training and learning opportunities do I anticipate for myself?	What is the theory of learning, if there is one? How many participants are enrolled in each course? What opportunities does the program offer for advanced learning?
Coaching Practice	How much coaching practice do I want as part of the program?	What is the requirement for number of coaching clients? Number of coaching hours?
FOCUS ON DEVELOPING YOURSELF		
Self-transformation	To what degree am I looking for self-transformation? Am I ready to work on myself?	To what extent does the program focus on personal development? Will I be paid for coaching clients during the training?

Receive Coaching	What level of coaching or mentor support do I want from the program?	How many hours of coaching will I receive as part of the program?
		Am I able to choose my coach, or will he or she be assigned to me?
		Will I work with a peer coach or an experienced coach?
COACHING CERTIFICATION AND REPUTATION		
Credential	How important is it that a program offers a certificate or certification?	Does the program offer a certification or certificate? If so, what type of certification or certificate will I receive upon completion?
	How important is it that a program be accredited? Do I have a preference for the accreditation organization?	What coaching association(s), if any, are you affiliated with?
		How is the program set up to help me get credentialed from a coaching association?
Reputation in the Marketplace	How important is reputation to me?	What is the reputation of the program in the coaching community?
	How important is reputation to my target clients?	What is the reputation of the program within my target client demographic?

Affiliations	Are there any affiliations or connections that I hope to access through a program?	What affiliations does the program have and what benefits are provided to program participants/graduates?
PROGRAM LOGISTICS AND INVESTMENT		
Virtual or In Person	How do I like to learn? What learning format best supports my needs? What type of program works best with my schedule (e.g., virtual, in-person, monthly, weekends, weekdays)?	How is the program delivered? What parts of the program are online and what parts are in person? Are the days and times set, or are they flexible?
Location of Training	Do I have the time, money, and resources to travel to the program location? How will doing a local program affect my coaching goals?	Where is the training offered? How does the location impact the training, if at all?
Time and Effort Required	How much time do I have to dedicate to a program? Is now the right time to enroll in a coach training program?	What is the duration of the entire program? Are there accelerated options available? How much time does the program involve (inside and outside of class)? How many clients will I be required to coach and for how many hours?

Cost	What is my price range (considering the payoff of finding clients to coach during and/or after the program)?	How much does the program cost? Are payment plans available? What is included in and what is excluded from the price of tuition? If applicable, what is the average cost of travel to or from the in-person trainings?
THE BUSINESS OF COACHING		
Support to Launch a Coaching Business	How important is it for me to learn how to start a coaching practice as part of the program? What tools and resources do I need to support my coaching practice?	What level of business development training does the program provide? What support is offered to launch a coaching business?

PART V
COACHING RESOURCES

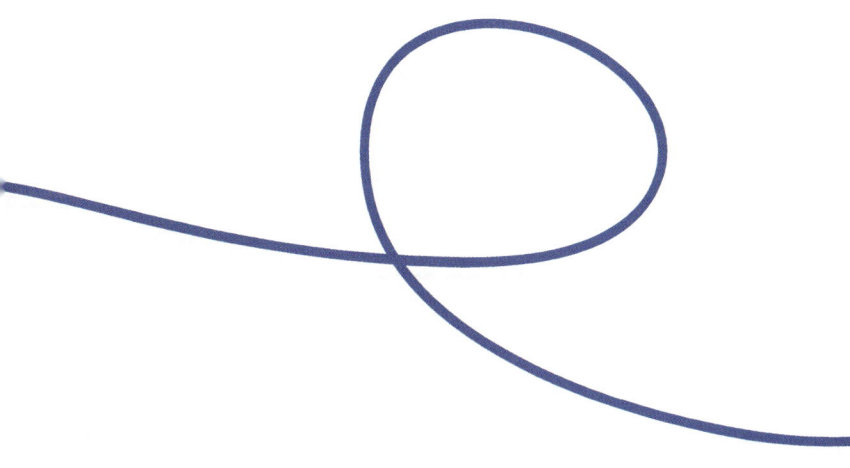

PART V

In Part V, I expand on the various coaching organizations and resources available to you in the form of websites, magazines, and books. There is no shortage of resources, and I have done the initial sorting to help you along your coaching journey.

COACHING ASSOCIATIONS AND ORGANIZATIONS

There are many coaching "tribes" in the form of associations and organizations that provide access to likeminded coaches and people with similar interests. These associations and organizations may offer immediate perks such as local and virtual networks or chapters that hold networking and educational events. Membership provides resources and other benefits such as listing your coaching practice for potential clients and engaging in a community of practice. The size of the community may vary and there are pros and cons to consider in being a part of a larger, more global network or a smaller, more intimate network. Also, note that you don't necessarily need to be credentialed by the association to become a member.

I've expanded on the organizations listed below.

- International Coach Federation (ICF)
- International Association of Coaching (IAC)
- Worldwide Association of Business Coaches (WABC)
- Center for Credentialing and Education (CCE)
- Institute of Coaching Professional Association (ICPA)

INTERNATIONAL COACH FEDERATION (ICF)

The International Coach Federation (ICF) is a globally recognized organization that provides both individual credentialing and program accreditation. It is headquartered in the United States with Regional Service Centers in Europe, Asia Pacific, and Latin America. The ICF supports all types of professional coaches. As of October 2013, ICF has 21,294 members in 110 countries and 11,311 credentialed coaches.

Note: *Coaches select ICF because it is a globally recognized association that is known by organizations. Coaches also choose ICF because they agree with its competency model, code of ethics, and credentialing process.*

Individual Credentialing:

There are three levels of credentials:

- Associate Certified Coach (ACC) – 100 hours of client coaching experience (for the practiced coach)
- Professional Certified Coach (PCC) – 750 hours of client coaching experience (for the proven coach)
- Master Certified Coach (MCC) – 2,500 hours of client coaching experience (for the expert coach)

If you decide that you want to become credentialed by the ICF, then you will need to apply even if you have attended an accredited ICF coach training program. However, if you have completed an accredited program (more on that follows), you will have already finished a portion of the requirements, which will give you a jump-start on your application. To keep your credential up-to-date, you will need to invest in continuing coach education (CCE) training and pay regular dues.

Program Accreditation:

The ICF has two different types of accreditation:

- Accredited Coach Training Program (ACTP)
- Approved Coach Specific Training Hours (ACSTH)

Programs that have ACTP status teach to the ICF Core competencies, its code of ethics, and its definition of coaching. ACTP programs also follow specific standards such as providing mentor coaches who share feedback on coach sessions and a final exam. By attending an ACTP program, it is easier to apply for the ICF credential because you will have partially completed the requirements.

On the other hand, if you've already completed an ACSTH program or other coach training courses, you can add up the total number of "student contact hours" and apply for an ICF credential using the portfolio path. Some programs will explicitly state that they teach you coaching skills at the ACC level or PCC level. What that means is that you receive more training hours, as there are more training hours required at the higher level of ICF credentials.

www.coachfederation.org

INTERNATIONAL ASSOCIATION OF COACHING (IAC)

The International Association of Coaching (IAC) is a globally recognized organization that provides individual credentialing and program licensing. It is based in the United States and supports all types of professional coaches. As of October 2013, IAC has approximately 1,000 members and more than 75 certified coaches.

Note: *Coaches select IAC because they agree with IAC's philosophy that you can be a great coach without needing to go through a coach training program. Rather, it's about mastery of IAC's coaching competencies and the ability to be a lifelong learner.*

Individual Credentialing:

There are two levels of certification:

- Skilled Certified Masteries Coach (CMC) - for experienced coaches
- Master Masteries Coach (MMC) - for expert coaches

There is also an IAC Masteries Practitioner, which is a learning designation for coaches who are working to apply and embody the IAC Masteries.

You are not required to have completed specific coach training in order to apply for IAC's certification. You will need to pass an online test that covers the IAC's nine coaching masteries as well as agree to the legal and ethical requirements. You must also submit recorded coaching sessions, which are evaluated by a certifying board. To stay certified, you will need to complete a learning agreement, which documents your personal plan to learn as a coach and pay regular dues.

Licensing of Organizations:

The IAC does not accredit organizations, but rather authorizes coach mentors and training programs to coach to its nine coaching masteries.

www.certifiedcoach.org

WORLDWIDE ASSOCIATION OF BUSINESS COACHES (WABC)

The Worldwide Association of Business Coaches (WABC) is a globally recognized organization that offers qualifications to individual business coaches (designations and degrees) and business coach training programs (accreditation). It is based in Canada and is independently owned. Its focus and differentiator is that it supports professional business coaches (as opposed to personal/professional coaches) who work in organizational and business contexts. As of October 2013, WABC has approximately 1,000 members in 30 countries and has awarded qualifications to more than 2,000 coaches.

Note: *Coaches select WABC because they are doing business coaching and are looking for a supportive community of coaches who do similar work within organizations.*

Individual Credentialing:

For a business coach to earn a qualification from WABC, you have to first be eligible for a WABC membership. The WABC membership includes a code of business coaching ethics, standards, and also requirements around work experience in the business, public, and/or nonprofit sectors. You also need to have completed the appropriate requirements leading to the qualification, which is the completion of either a program accredited by the WABC (more on that follows) or the completion of an independent portfolio.

There are different levels of qualifications for business coaches:

- Non-Certification Designation / Registered Corporate Coach™ (RCC™) - for individuals who have business coaching experience but haven't received formal training
- Certification Designation / WABC Certified Business Coach™ (CBC™) - for practitioner-level business coaches
- Certification Designation / WABC Certified Master Business Coach™ (CMBC™) - for master-level business coaches
- Certification Designation / Chartered Business Coach™ (ChBC™) - for senior-level professional business coaches

The WABC also has two fully accredited academic degree options, which are awarded by Middlesex University in the

United Kingdom: the Master of Arts in Professional Development (Business Coaching) and the Doctorate in Professional Studies (Business Coaching).

Program Accreditation:

The WABC offers four levels of program accreditation for business coaching training programs:

- WABC Accredited (Level 1 – RCC™)
- WABC Accredited (Level 2 – CBC™)
- WABC Accredited (Level 3 – CMBC™)
- WABC Accredited (Level 4 – ChBC™)

Programs that are accredited by WABC will differ in length of duration as well as the total number of learning hours and faculty required.

www.wabccoaches.com

CENTER FOR CREDENTIALING AND EDUCATION (CCE)

The Center for Credentialing and Education (CCE) is based in the United States and serves organizations, professionals, and the public in credentialing, ethics, assessment, and organizational management. CCE offers seven credentials that range from clinical supervision to counseling and facilitation, and as of 2011, it added coaching to its existing certification offerings. As of September 2013, CCE has more than 2,400 certified coaches through its Board Certified Coach (BCC) designation.

Note: *Coaches often select CCE because of their backgrounds in therapy or counseling and have familiarity with the organization given its experience in credentialing.*

Individual Credentialing:

CCE offers the Board Certified Coach as an individual credential. The training requirements vary based on your academic degree and your experience in coaching. At a minimum, you will need to have completed a bachelor's degree and 30 hours of coaching and training. As you apply for the credential, you will need to submit proof that you have done coach training from a CCE-approved training provider as well as pass a written exam, submit an endorsement, and pay a fee.

The BCC credential has four coaching specialty designations: Executive/Corporate/Business/Leadership Coach, Health and Wellness Coach, Career Coach, and Personal/Life Coach.

Approval of Coach Training Programs:

CCE does not accredit programs, but rather approves coach training programs based on its criteria. The approved programs are known as CCE-Approved Board Certified Coach Training Providers.

www.cce-global.org

INSTITUTE OF COACHING PROFESSIONAL ASSOCIATION (ICPA)

The Institute of Coaching at McLean Hospital is an affiliate of Harvard Medical School and is a nonprofit organization. ICPA has five centers—Research, Education, Coaching in Leadership, Coaching in Healthcare, and Applied Positive Psychology. Through its Center for Research, ICPA advances coaching research by providing grant funding for coaching. You can join the ICPA by making a donation. Membership gives you access to resources, networks, and learning opportunities. As of September 2013, ICPA has more than 1,150 members.

Note: *Coaches look to ICPA as a leading source of evidence-based research. You can apply for a grant through the ICPA, become a member of the network, and also gain access to coaching contacts and content.*

www.instituteofcoaching.org

ORGANIZATIONS THAT SUPPORT COACH TRAINING/EDUCATION

There are also organizations that serve coach training and education. I've expanded on these organizations below so that you are aware of how they can support you.

- Graduate School Alliance for Executive Coaching (GSAEC)
- Association of Coach Training Organizations (ACTO)

GRADUATE SCHOOL ALLIANCE FOR EXECUTIVE COACHING (GSAEC)

GSAEC is an organization that supports and strengthens the practice of executive and organizational coaching in academic institutions. GSAEC sets and maintains academic standards for graduate education programs that focus on executive and organizational coaching. GSAEC has institutional membership for schools and training programs and also offers an individual membership for people interested in executive, organizational, or leadership coaching.

Note: *If you're interested in coaching through an academics-focused or evidence-based lens, GSAEC is a great place to start your research on graduate-level programs that incorporate coaching.*

www.gsaec.org

ASSOCIATION OF COACH TRAINING ORGANIZATIONS (ACTO)

ACTO serves as a collaboration hub for coach education and training. The organization helps coach training programs share best practices and support one another. It also furthers the profession of coaching by defining its body of knowledge and advocating for students and graduates.

You can look at ACTO to see which coach training programs have decided to become ACTO members, although note that a lot of International Coach Federation (ICF) accredited programs comprise this organization given that it emerged from ICF member schools.

www.actoonline.org

WEBSITES AND MAGAZINES

I have shared websites and magazines that are specifically designed for coaches to stay relevant and informed, although they may also cover other topics as well, such as how to coach, tools to support you in coaching, and how to brand and market your business.

I've expanded on the websites and magazines listed below.

- Peer Resources – Peer, Mentor and Coach Resources
- Library of Professional Coaching (LPC)

- *Choice*, the magazine of professional coaching

PEER RESOURCES NETWORK

Peer Resources Network is a website with information on peer, coach, and mentor programs as well as coaching, events, and more. While you can peruse content for free, becoming a member of Peer Resources provides access to the broader website and perks such as the monthly Peer Resources Bulletin, which includes relevant coaching articles and access to coaching request for proposals (RFPs).

Note: *Peer Resources is an ideal place to start to learn more about coach training programs, accreditation, and other resources that you should know about as a coach. While the site can be challenging to navigate, the content and expertise is extensive.*

www.peer.ca

THE LIBRARY OF PROFESSIONAL COACHING (LPC)

The Library of Professional Coaching has free resources in the form of relevant articles, research, and white papers on professional coaching. The website has recently started offering a digital magazine. There is no cost to submit articles directly to the Library of Professional Coaching, and it can be a place for you as a coach to publish your research and articles.

Note: *The Library of Professional Coaching has categorized and tagged various coaching theories and concepts that are easily searchable. This is a useful site to learn about different topics in coaching that might interest you and be able to search relevant articles.*

www.libraryofprofessionalcoaching.com

CHOICE, THE MAGAZINE OF PROFESSIONAL COACHING

Choice is a quarterly published magazine that is offered in print and digitally. *Choice* magazine also offers a membership component called CIM: Choice Interactive Membership. It includes an online forum and resources for coaches.

Note: *Choice magazine is a fun and engaging read for coaches who want to stay up-to-date about the latest trends in the coaching field. Its website has additional resources to help you get started in coaching and eventually in growing and developing your practice.*

www.choice-online.com

BOOKS

How to Become a Coach
ebook (Bond)
www.how-to-become-a-coach.com

Coaching Skills: A Handbook (Rogers)

The Completely Revised Handbook of Coaching: A Developmental Approach (McLean)

Immunity to Change: How to Overcome It and Unlock the Potential in Yourself and Your Organization (Lahey and Kegan)

What Got You Here Won't Get You There: How Successful People Become Even More Successful (Goldsmith, Reiter)

Organizational Coaching: Building Relationships and Programs that Drive Results (Bianco-Mathis, Roman, Nabors)

Executive Coaching with Backbone and Heart: A Systems Approach to Engaging Leaders with Their Challenges (O'Neill)

For more book recommendations, please visit **www.coachingiscalling.com**.

COACH TRAINING PROGRAMS

I have included the list of coach training programs that I researched, as well as their marquee, or signature, book that highlights the thinking of its early coach founders and leaders. If you're considering a coach training program, this is a useful place to start to learn about each program's philosophy, models/frameworks, methodologies, and tools/templates.

Please note that there are other coach training programs that are not included in this list.

Organization: **Accomplishment Coaching**
Program: Coach Training Program
Certification/Certificate: Accomplishment Coach
Must-Read Book/Article or Website:
www.accomplishmentcoaching.com

Organization: **Center for Presence-Based Leadership Development**
Program: Presence-Based Coach Training/Certification
Certification/Certificate: Presence-Based Coach
Must-Read Book/Article or Website: *Presence-Based Coaching* (Silsbee)

Organization: **Coach Inc.: Coach U and Corporate Coach U**
Program: Advanced Coaching Program™ (ACP™)
Certification/Certificate: Coach U Certified Graduate (CUCG)

Corporate Coach U Certified Graduate (CCUCG)
Must-Read Book/Article or Website: www.coachinc.com

Organization: **Coach For Life**
Program: Certified Life Coach Program™ and Master Certified Life Coach Program™
Certification/Certificate: Certified Life Coach (CLC) and Master Certified Life Coach (MCLC)
Must-Read Book/Article or Website: *Positively Brilliant Self-mastery: Reclaim Your Authentic Self Now* (Reding)

Organization: **The Coaches Training Institute (CTI)**
Program: Co-Active Coach Training Program
Certification/Certificate: Certified Professional Co-Active Coach (CPCC)
Must-Read Book/Article or Website: *Co-Active Coaching: Changing Business, Transforming Lives* (Whitworth, K. Kimsey-House, H. Kimsey-House, Sandahl)

Organization: **Columbia University**
Program: Columbia Coaching Certification Program (CCCP)
Certification/Certificate: Certified Columbia Coach
Must-Read Book/Article or Website: www.tc.columbia.edu/coachingcertification/

Organization: **CRR Global**
Program: ORSC Coaching Certification Program
Certification/Certificate: Certified ORSC Coach
Must-Read Book/Article or Website: www.crrglobal.com

Organization: **Georgetown University**
Program: Institute for Transformational Leadership
Certification/Certificate: Certificate in Leadership Coaching
Must-Read Book/Article or Website: *On Becoming a Leadership Coach: A Holistic Approach to Coaching Excellence* (Bloomfield, Wahl, Scriber)

Organization: **Hudson Institute of Coaching**
Program: Coach Certification Program
Certification/Certificate: Professional Certification in Leadership Coaching & Transition Coaching
Must-Read Book/Article or Website: *The Adult Years: Mastering the Art of Self-Renewal* (Hudson)

Organization: **Integral Coaching Canada Inc.**
Program: Integral Coaching Certification Program (ICCP)
Certification/Certificate: Integral Master Coach™
Must-Read Book/Article or Website: Spring 2009 Integral Coaching issue of the *Journal of Integral Theory and Practice*

Organization: **Institute of Life Coach Training**
Program: Credentialing Path / Specialties Path / Self-Directed Courses
Certification/Certificate: Certified Life Coach (CLC) credential
Must-Read Book/Article or Website: *Becoming a Professional Life Coach: Lessons from the Institute of Life Coach Training* (Menendez, Williams)

Organization: **iPEC**
Program: Coach Certification Program
Certification/Certificate: Certified Professional Coach (CPC) and Energy Leadership Index™ Master Practitioner (ELI-MP)
Must-Read Book/Article or Website: *Energy Leadership: Transforming Your Workplace and Your Life from the Core* (Schneider)

Organization: **Martha Beck**
Program: Life Coach Training
Certification/Certificate: Certified Martha Beck Life Coach
Must-Read Book/Article or Website: *Finding Your Own North Star: Claiming the Life You Were Meant to Live* (Beck)

Organization: **NeuroLeadership Group**
Program: Brain-Based coach training programs
Certification/Certificate: Result Brain-Based Coaching Certificate
Must-Read Book/Article or Website: *Quiet Leadership: Six Steps for Transforming Performance at Work* (Rock)

Organization: **Newfield Network**
Program: Certified Coach Training
Certification/Certificate: Certified Ontological Coach
Must-Read Book/Article or Website:
www.newfieldnetwork.com

Organization: **New Ventures West**
Program: Professional Coaching Course
Certification/Certificate: Certified Integral Coach
Must-Read Book/Article or Website: *Coaching: Evoking Excellence in Others* (Flaherty)

Organization: **Strozzi Institute**
Program: Strozzi Institute Somatic Coach (SISC) Certification
Certification/Certificate: Strozzi Institute Somatic Coach
Must-Read Book/Article or Website: *Holding the Center: Sanctuary in a Time of Confusion* (Strozzi Heckler)

Organization: **The University of Texas at Dallas School of Management**
Program: Executive and Professional Certificate Program
Certification/Certificate: Graduate Certificate in Coaching
Must-Read Book/Article or Website:
www.jindal.utdallas.edu/executive-education/organizational-behavior-and-executive-coaching/

CONCLUSION

CONCLUSION

Your answers to the questions in Coaching is Calling *will evolve over time. This book can serve as a reference to come back to as you discover what's important to you on your developmental path. It can also help as you define who you are as a coach.*

Let's review where we have gone together. In Part I, you were introduced to the coaching journey and what you may start to think about on your developmental path. Part II elaborated on what you need to know about coaching and provided a framework for understanding the different types of coaches and career paths. Parts III and IV discussed the considerations for selecting coach training programs and identifying the best fit for you. Part V expanded on the coaching associations and resources available.

By taking the time to answer the worksheets and Pause reflections, you will have gained additional clarity about who you are and what is calling you to coaching. Perhaps you have articulated more clearly what it is that you want out of a coach training program and the type of coaching that excites you. Whatever you are taking with you is enough. What's important is how you want to move forward with the insights you've gained.

Also, you may have a sense of the diversity of backgrounds and experiences that the coaches mentioned in *Coaching is Calling* have. These coaches are big-hearted and magnetic people. They carry a joy of living that is not always easily found in others. Their stories are rich and intricate, and these snapshots are only a glimpse into their lives. As you get to know more coaches, you'll encounter the generosity of spirit that made this book possible.

I hope that you too can channel this sense of personal joy in the art of coaching and share it with others. Through coaching, you will have the ability to change yourself and the world around you. So, where do you want to begin?

For more information on Coaching is Calling, *visit* **www.coachingiscalling.com**.

ABOUT THE AUTHOR

Lauren B. Weinstein is passionate about coaching as a tool for change and is committed to working with organizations seeking positive social impact in the world.

Previously, Lauren spent seven years at Accenture, where she worked primarily in Corporate Social Responsibility and International Development through Accenture Development Partnerships (ADP), a group that employs an innovative not-for-profit business model to make Accenture services accessible to the international development sector.

Lauren has a BA in Communications from the University of Pennsylvania. She has a Certification in Leadership Coaching from Georgetown University. Lauren has completed Hudson Institute of Coaching's LifeLaunch and the Strozzi Institute's Leadership in Action 1. Lauren is a StartingBloc Fellow and a Net Impact Professional Member.

Learn more about Lauren at **www.laurenbweinstein.com**.

NOTES

Made in the USA
Lexington, KY
17 April 2014